DRAWING FANTASTIC

Dragons

DRAWING FANTASTIC

Dragons

Sandra Staple

Create Amazing Full-Color Dragon Art, Including
Eastern, Western and Classic Beasts

Ulysses Press

Published in the United States by:
Ulysses Press
P.O. Box 3440
Berkeley, CA 94703
www.ulyssespress.com

ISBN: 978-1-61243-761-3
Library of Congress Control Number 2017952128

Printed in Korea by Artin Printing through Four Colour Print Group
10 9 8 7 6 5 4 3 2 1

Acquisitions editor: Casie Vogel
Managing editor: Claire Chun
Editor: Renee Rutledge
Proofreader: Shayna Keyles
Front cover design: Justin Shirley
Cover art: Sandra Staple; parchment background © Sk_Advance studio/shuttersstock.com
Interior art: Sandra Staple

Distributed by Publishers Group West

When my now 10-year-old daughter, Chloe, was 18 months old, she was diagnosed with type 1 diabetes. So I would like to dedicate this book to her, and all the teens and children out there fighting against these types of illnesses that so quickly take over a large part of their lives. To me, they are stronger, braver, and more courageous than any dragon in this book could be!

Acknowledgments

First, I would like to thank my husband, Jason, for without his strong support and encouragement to pursue my artistic career, this book certainly would not have happened. I would also like to thank all my friends and family, who offered great moral support when I quit my career as a business analyst. Finally, I would like to thank everyone I worked with at Ulysses Press, who were endlessly patient while I worked on all the drawings for this book. Thank you everyone for making this project a success!

Contents

Introduction   1

Section 1
DRAWING AND COLORING BASICS   3

Section 2
DRAWING THE DRAGON BODY AND FORM   11

Section 3
CREATING DISTINCTIVE DRAGONS WITH PERSONALITY   57

Section 4
UNIQUE DRAGONS AND CLASSIC BEASTS   95

Last Words   137

About the Author   138

Introduction

With so many mediums that an artist can work with today, it can be hard to decide which one to choose! Picking up pencils and paper is a great start for any young artist, and these tools are versatile, inexpensive, and mobile as well. Bring a sketchpad and a few pencils with you before heading out to a park or to your next movie night at a friend's house. (That way, if you end up watching a truly terrible movie but manage to draw something you like, the evening isn't totally wasted!) I used to bring a 24-pack of colored pencils with me and even kept a box at my desk at some of my first jobs for when there was downtime (shh!).

Drawing is a great hobby to help escape the busy and hectic schedules many of us face each day, whether at work or at school, and it allows some quiet time for the mind to wander. I often listen to music while I draw, but will sometimes just enjoy the quiet, allowing my mind to imagine wonderful stories for the characters and creatures I am creating.

Drawing creatures such as dragons allows you to really stretch your imagination, since there are no photos that you must follow exactly in order to create a realistic creature. If you look at the vast amount of dragon art created over years of our fascination with the beast, you will find so much variance between them that they could be separate creatures altogether. So my request to you is, as you follow through this book, try to also find and embrace your own style of art and your own style of dragon, and don't become discouraged if your pieces don't turn out just like mine. Allow yourself to make mistakes without being discouraged, and most importantly, keep practicing! You will be surprised at how quickly you improve if you just keep on drawing.

Section 1
DRAWING AND COLORING BASICS

Before you get started, you will need to acquire some basic tools and learn some simple tips and techniques in order to create your finished works of art.

Although you can technically pick up any cheap pencil and notepad, I strongly advise against them, especially loose-leaf books or lined notebooks. I had a young fan visit me for her birthday one year. Her parents had surprised her by buying her a copy of my book because she had taken it out of the library so many times to draw from, and since they lived nearby, they brought her over with the book so I could sign it. She showed me her sketchbook, and although it is always nice to see new work from a budding artist, I cringed when I saw that her sketchbook was actually a lined paper notebook. It greatly takes away from your drawing to have lines going through it. (Of course this will happen when you inevitably doodle through a boring class or long day of work, but it shouldn't be in your main sketchbook or on your main drawings.) The first thing I told her parents were—you guessed it—get her a proper sketchbook!

So if you take one thing away from this entire section, GET A NICE SKETCHBOOK! See, I even capitalized it so you can't say you didn't see that if you turned to this page. It doesn't even have to be a super nice one, just one that has white paper. I would advise against getting a brown-hued or newsprint pad. Try to at least get something that has white sheets in it so that the paper color doesn't influence the colors of your drawing. Getting a sketch pad with acid-free paper would also be a bonus, as then your paper won't turn yellow over time, which is why I don't recommend drawing on regular computer printer paper (except for those doodles at the office or at school, when there is no other white paper to turn to!).

TOOLS OF THE TRADE

Other than the medium you choose to color your drawings with, I would say there are five essential things you need before you get started sketching, plus one item that is nice to have.

PAPER/SKETCHBOOKS

As I already mentioned, get yourself a nice, acid-free, unlined sketchbook or notepad with white paper to draw in. I recommend getting something around 8 x 10 inches in size, as it's a standard size to work with. It gives you enough room to draw something large, and it also fits nicely on your lap. I actually prefer the coiled, hardcover sketchbooks, as these can be folded all the way around, and the hardcover makes it easy to draw without having to sit at a table or desk.

PENCILS

Regardless of what medium you are planning to color your final drawing in, your initial sketch will probably be done using a pencil. Unless you have a really nice tablet, of course, but there are no plugs at the beach (if you plan on drawing there), and it's sandy there, so I usually recommend something less risky, like a sketchbook and pencil. You don't need to get a really expensive set of pencils, but you will find a difference between a cheap pencil and an artist's one. Most small artist's pencil sets aren't too expensive, and you can often pick them up at large retailers like Walmart. For sketching I usually use a B or HB pencil, and then for my final drawing (I like to trace my sketch onto a new piece of paper), I usually use HB or H, with a very sharp tip. Keep in mind, it's important to press lightly when using these harder pencils, so as not to dent the paper or have lines show up on the final colored version.

SHARPENERS

Get yourself a good sharpener; otherwise, you'll find you're constantly breaking your pencils just trying to sharpen them! And once your sharpener is dull, make sure you get a new one.

SMUDGE STICKS/BLENDERS

In my previous book, *Drawing Dragons*, I explained how to use a smudge stick for graphite pencil drawings. For colored pencils, you can buy what's called a colorless blender to blend your colors together. Or, you can buy lots of white pencils. I use a white colored pencil for blending more often than anything else. (I think I used up about six or seven white pencils just doing the artwork for this book!)

ERASERS

A good eraser is a must! In fact, I recommend buying a few, if you can swing it. I like the large, white, gum erasers for sketching over large areas; an eraser pencil (a pencil with an eraser core you can sharpen) for fine details; and an electric eraser for those hard-to-remove colored pencil areas on the finished drawing (they are surprisingly cheap!).

LIGHT TABLE

A light table is simply a box with a translucent piece of flat plastic on the top and a light source inside, such as short fluorescent tubes. Drawing on top of this tool makes it easy to copy a rough drawing or sketch onto a new piece of paper. If you don't have one, you can get a similar effect by holding your drawings up to a window when it's light outside.

CHOOSING YOUR MEDIUM

The medium you choose for coloring your finished drawings in is an entirely personal choice. Or, you may prefer leaving some of your drawings black and white. (My previous book is done entirely in graphite pencil and has many fully finished pieces that look great in grayscale.) Let's take a look at some (but not all, as there are just too many) of the choices you have for coloring your art.

The mediums we are going to look at here are relatively affordable and portable. So while oil painting is a wonderful medium, it isn't really easy to just grab a canvas board, tons of expensive tubes of oil paint, and set off to paint, especially since cleanup can't be done with just water. And digital is wonderful too, but again, you will need a pricey tablet, drawing software, and a power source to plug it into. So we are going to step back (in time, maybe?) and look at some simpler options an artist may choose.

COLORED PENCILS

This is one of my favorite mediums to work in. It is versatile, relatively inexpensive, and easily portable. I will often carry a piece of art I have already finished sketching, along with the colors I am going to use in a pencil case (for example, when working on the green dragon on page 2, I brought a selection of greens, yellows, and browns). Colored pencil has the advantage of being a relatively mess-free medium and also allows for a great level of detail in your work.

WATERCOLOR PAINT

This is another one of my favorites. It is a little more portable than other paints because it air-dries quickly, cleans up with water, and doesn't have to be cleaned off your pallet. I never wash away unused watercolor paint because once it dries up, you can use it again later by reapplying water. Watercolor can be a trickier medium to master, especially when doing detailed pieces, but is also a fun one to play around with. This little watercolor dragon example was painted using very cheap puck paints. For a more detailed watercolor example, check out the green dragon on the acknowledgments page at the beginning of the book.

ACRYLIC PAINT

Though the least portable of the mediums mentioned here, acrylic paint does at least clean up with water. One of the advantages to painting with acrylics is that once the paint dries, it stays dry, so you can layer it on (similar to oil paint), making it easier to cover up an area of your art that needs fixing. You can use acrylic in a similar style to watercolor by watering it down, but once it dries, it stays dry. You can also paint with it more thickly, as I did with this little dragon, layering the pattern right on top of the first layer of paint.

OIL PASTELS

Although oil pastels are very portable, I rarely use it for drawing, as it can be quite messy and hard to create details with. However, it is fun to use for larger, less detailed pieces, and it creates very vibrant, stunning colors. For the example here, it was quite difficult to get any details on my small dragon, but the colors were very bright.

CHALK PASTELS

Chalk pastels can be fun to use and are fairly portable. Although they are a bit messy, they clean up easier than oil pastels. They are similar to oil pastels in the sense that they can be hard to create a high level of detail with, but are very different in that they tend to create softer, more muted pieces. The little dragon I colored with chalk pastel turned out quite muted, as it was hard to get darker colors.

Once you have chosen your medium, you can get started coloring! For this book, I mostly used colored pencil, as I feel it is the most practical medium for learning, and also a great medium for experienced artists. (And, yes, my little colored pencil dragon on these pages is my favorite out of the five examples!)

CONTEXT

When sitting down to plan out a drawing, you need to consider exactly what you want to portray. A dragon on its own may give a certain mood to a drawing, but what type of environment you put it in, and what type of colors and props you use in your drawing, can greatly alter that.

For example, a drawing of a large dragon rearing up and roaring, surrounded by a half-destroyed castle lit up in flames, portrays a destructive, dangerous dragon causing havoc. But if you took that exact same dragon, in the exact same roaring, menacing pose, then drew a few little baby dragons hidden behind its legs and tail, suddenly the context of the dragon changes dramatically from terrifying menace to protective parent.

Let's take a look at an example here. I drew a red dragon crouched and roaring. Now I must decide.... who exactly is he roaring at? Is he on the defensive or offensive? How big is he?

In the first illustration, below, he is a huge, red dragon being attacked by (or perhaps attacking) a small group of knights. The knights don't have much chance of hurting him. If anything, they look like they are delivering nice, bite-sized horses for his munching pleasure.

This wasn't really how I wanted to portray this dragon, though, so in the end I scrapped that idea. Instead, as you can see on the next page, I drew him hidden in some glowing red leaves, facing off with what I would consider to be an actual threat to him—a large wasp. Now, yes, the dragon is certainly a lot larger than the wasp. But wasps are fast. And territorial. And mean. And they will sting you over and over. (Yes, I hate wasps.) A wasp can make my 75-pound, muscle-bound dog go running to her bed with her tail between her legs (she has been stung before and now will run in the house if you even say the word "wasp!"), so I'm sure this little red dragon would be worried. Perhaps he is attacking the wasp, but

perhaps he is just going "Oh, crap!" and slowly, slowly backing away from the black and yellow terror bug.

So there is the same dragon in two very different scenes that totally changes the entire context of the piece! Think of that when drawing and sketching your dragons. You drew a dragon, now what exactly is going on with that dragon? Your picture can tell a very different story depending on how you choose to show it.

TIP: IMPROVING YOUR SKETCH

When you're not just doodling on the side of a notebook (or test; I used to do that on my math tests in the tenth grade, as I would usually finish early and then turn my graphs into little scenes) and you are purposely sitting down to sketch, you are usually committing to trying to create something more substantial than a blocky dragon doodle.

My recommendation for sketching is to try to improve, rather than always sketching what you already know how to draw. For example, if you have an idea of what you want to draw, try to have a book, magazine, or photo handy for references, or turn to the internet. I don't mean copying, but just trying to improve. You would be surprised at how flawed your memory of what something looks like can be if you're always trying to draw it out of your head!

Section 2

DRAWING THE DRAGON BODY AND FORM

Now that you have taken a look at some drawing concepts and decided on colored pencil as your medium, you can get to the fun part—actually drawing a dragon!

But wait...before you jump right in and start drawing a whole dragon, you need to look at the different parts that will make up your amazing beast.

One of the great things about drawing dragons is that you can pretty much draw them however you want to. That being said, there are certain features that tend to be common when drawing dragons, without which your dragonish monster will just end up looking like a flying dog or a big, winged, air-breathing fish of doom.

In order to prevent the fish-of-doom scenario, let's take a look at some of the common body parts and body types you can give your dragon. From there, you can choose the customizations that suit you.

DRAGON EYES

The type of eyes you choose to draw on your dragon can have a huge impact on the dragon's mood and personality. Let's take a look at drawing a basic dragon eye, and then at some of the types of eyes you can draw.

1 Draw a basic eye shape. It's kind of like a lemon, only it turns down a bit on one end. Fill in the iris and pupil of your eye.

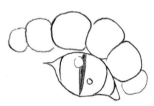

2 Fill in some more details around the pupil, iris, eyelid, and tear duct. Now you have your basic eye finished; if there is anything at this point you are not happy with, you can fix it in the next step when you copy it over to new paper. Start the eye ridge (the area above the basic eye shape) as it can have a big effect on what type of mood your dragon looks to be in.

3 If you were just designing a rough draft of your drawing and now copying over to a new piece of paper, fix any details you are not happy with, and fill in a few more details in the iris. In this example, I added a darker shadow to the top of the eye.

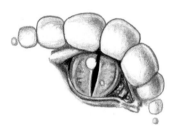

4 Add your colors, keeping in mind whether or not you want white to show in the sclera (the white part of the human eye). Add darker colors underneath the lid and eye ridge.

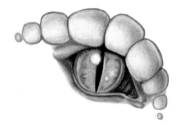

5 Blend your colors. In this example, I blended the colors using a white-colored pencil and a colorless blender for the pupil and black shadows under the eye ridge.

6 Darken up your colors again. Additional color goes on smoothly after the white blending. Add some highlights to the eye; I used white to add highlights to the iris so it appears glossy, and an electric eraser to clean up the highlights.

TYPES OF EYES

I will often change the type of eye I give my dragon depending on the personality I want it to have, and sometimes even depending on the size of the drawing. The smaller the drawing, the harder it is to get any detail in the eye!

Let's take a look at some eye types you can give your dragon. Of course, you can always take some features from a few different eyes to create your own dragon eye.

HUMAN EYE

This is probably the eye you are most familiar with! It is easy to find subjects to model for you when drawing this eye, if you are looking for different angles. It's a good eye to use if you want your dragon to appear wise and intelligent.

LION EYE

Lion eyes actually have round pupils, unlike tigers. This is a great choice for a dragon that you want to portray as being more benevolent, but still a fierce hunter.

SNAKE EYE

The slit eye of a snake is one of my favorites to incorporate into a dragon's eye! Snake eyes don't usually have a noticeable lid or sclera.

HORSE EYE

Horse eyes have a wonderful, gentle, and kind shape and look to them. They have a dreamy, ethereal appearance and an unusually shaped pupil, as horses don't have binocular vision.

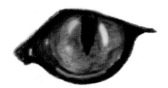

TIGER EYE

Tiger eyes are a great shape for portraying intelligence. They also have that dragonish pupil when contracted.

LIZARD EYE

Some lizards and frogs have very strange pupils, and wide, round eyes, which can really give a dragon an eerie, otherworldly look.

DRAGON EARS

Although a dragon's ears can seem like a minor detail, they really can make a big difference to the overall look of your dragon's face! If you want your dragon to appear cute and cuddly, for example, you may not want to give him giant horned and spiky ears! Likewise, a large, menacing, princess-eating beast probably shouldn't have fuzzy, floppy bunny ears (although that would be a good way to trick an unsuspecting princess into coming close enough to be eaten!).

Let's take a look at some types of ears you can give your cute and adorable—I mean, ferocious—beast!

RIBBED EAR

This ear has long, stiff spines that fan out, with softer tissue between, almost like tiny wings.

HORNED EAR

If you want to give your dragon a more menacing look, reminiscent of a dinosaur, replace the ears with long horns or spikes.

FAN EAR

The bottom of this ear fans out on its own, without any actual spines.

FEATHERED EAR

If your dragon has feathers, you may want to make the ears feathered too!

FURRY EAR

This is a great ear to use when drawing fuzzy, cute dragons, or really any dragon that has fur instead of scales.

BAT EAR

Bats have large, pointed ears so they can hunt their prey with deadly sonar precision. You can make these ears large or small.

DRAGON SNOUTS

Who knows what a dragon's nose looks like, exactly? Perhaps we can agree that a dragon's nose doesn't look like its toes, or a rose, I suppose? How your dragon's snout looks is entirely up to you! Let's take a look at some types of noses you can give your beast.

DRAGONISH SNOUT

This would be my standard dragon nose. I draw it on most (but not all) of my dragons. It resembles a beak but without a sharp hook, and with the nostrils at the end, like those on a horse's nose.

CAT NOSE

I often draw Eastern dragons with a more catlike nose and mouth, but you can give any dragon this nose. You can still make your dragon look menacing by adding large fangs.

ALLIGATOR SNOUT

This nose is longer, with a rounded snout on the end and lots of protruding teeth coming out of its mouth, which does not have to be straight.

LIZARD SNOUT

Lizards can have such varying noses and faces that if you are going for a particular type of lizard, I suggest you use a reference.

EAGLE BEAK

An eagle or hawk beak has a very sharp point on the end for tearing apart its food. The nostril is actually further up the beak, closer to the eyes, than in the previous examples.

HORSE MUZZLE

Horses have a long face, and the end of the face that includes the mouth and nostrils is called the muzzle. This is a great nose to use on kind, benevolent, non-meat-eating dragons.

DRAWING A DRAGON'S HEAD

You have taken a look at a few fundamental parts of a dragon's head, so now, try putting them all together to draw the whole thing! The initial shape you start your head with can have a huge effect on the overall look of your beast, so take some time when building your head to determine what your favorite head shape is. Perhaps you find you prefer drawing long-snouted, slender dragons, or you may find the opposite and that shorter, broader, muscle-bound dragons are more your style. Either way, it all begins with how you build your initial dragon's head.

I have always felt the head is the most important part when starting a dragon drawing, or really any animal at all. Its position, angle, and build will all impact your drawing. So take your time and don't rush this very important part of your dragon!

Let's take a look at three classic angles that are common to draw: front view, partial side view, and full side view. Once you have mastered the basic dragon head at these angels, you can start customizing them with different eyes, noses, ears, and other unique details.

THE DRAGON HEAD: FRONT PROFILE

When drawing a dragon facing you, you need to consider exactly how the dragon is holding its head, as this will have a great impact on the feel and mood of the dragon. For example, a dragon looking directly down his snout, causing you to look more at its nose than its eyes, could be either comical or intimidating depending on the expression (or if it looks like it's getting ready to eat you). In my first book, *Drawing Dragons*, we drew a dragon with his head pointed quite sternly downward (like the red dragon on page 10), so this time, let's take a look at a dragon looking straight at the viewer.

1 Start your dragon with the main skull circle, followed by a smaller nose circle, and then attach the two. The more downward the dragon's head is tilted, the farther away the nose circle will be from the larger skull circle. Because this dragon is looking forward and doesn't have its head lowered too much, we will draw the smaller circle so it actually overlaps the first circle.

2 Next, determine how you want the ears and neck positioned, as this will affect how you pose your dragon. Draw the basic ear shape you want, and draw the neck using flowing, curved lines. If you draw the neck lines too straight, your dragon neck will look more like a giraffe neck...or like a telephone pole!

3 Now you are ready to start adding your basic dragon facial features over your building lines. Start by shaping out the head and nose. This dragon is going to have a pointy, dragonish snout. Add your eyes, making sure they aren't too far down the dragon's face, or it will look like it has eyes on its snout. Don't draw them too high up either or they will look like they're on the dragon's forehead. The center of the eyes should be about two-thirds up the head.

4 Fill in the rest of the details of your dragon's head, including the rest of the ears, horns, eyebrows, etc. You can add scales now if you want to, or you can wait to add them later. Now you have finished designing your dragon head and are ready to either clean up the building lines or copy the drawing onto a new piece of paper.

5 I always recommend copying your rough drawing onto a new piece of paper if you can, but if you don't want to do that as you are keeping your drawing in a sketchbook, I would suggest lightly erasing over the entire drawing while completely erasing the building lines (such as the circles.) This allows you to then carefully go over the lines that you want to keep, cleaning up any details that need fixing before you start to color.

6 This is the first step in coloring your dragon. I usually start with two or three colors for my first layer of color. For this dragon, I used a medium blue, purple, and black. When shading with colored pencil, leave the areas you want to highlight white, as you will be blending into those areas in the next step.

7 Now, blend your colors together. Using a soft, white-colored pencil, blend the colors together over the entire piece to create a smooth texture. Don't worry that your colors get lightened up by the white. The next step will be to finish the drawing and darken them up, but the white blending will give a smooth surface to work with.

8 Darken up the shadows and areas that were lightened up too much by the white blending, and finish adding any details, such as scales, to the surface of your dragon. Your masterpiece is complete!

TIP: THE EASIEST LIGHT SOURCE IS A SOFT ONE

Try not to have a really stark light source, unless you have a reference photo or model to work with, as it can be harder to make the bright highlights look realistic and placed correctly on your dragon when you are just guessing as to how the light would be hitting the subject. There are entire art books dedicated to the subject! Think of how light appears on a cloudy day. You can still see what direction the light is coming from without having really bright white spots, sun spots, or dark shadows.

THE DRAGON HEAD: PARTIAL SIDE VIEW

This is my favorite angle from which to draw a dragon's head, as you can see a bit of the eye from the mostly hidden side of the face, and more of the forehead. It makes it more interesting when adding horns, fins, and ridges, because you can play around with the angle of the horns and show them more fully.

1 Start with a large circle for the skull and a smaller circle for the nose, and then connect them. The farther apart the two circles, the longer the dragon's face will be. Decide what type of ears you want and how to position them, then add the neck.

2 Draw out what type of shape you want the end of the dragon's face to have, and position the eyes. Because this is a partially tilted head, the mouth will be quite low on the face, and the eye will be around the middle of the face.

3 Fill in the remaining details such as nostrils, ears, pupils, horns, ridges, etc. The nostril should also be lower on the nose, not in the middle, because the head is tilted forward.

4 Copy your rough drawing onto a new piece of paper or clean up your building lines.

5 Decide what color you want to use and start building your color up. For this dragon we are going to go with a light source somewhat in front of the dragon, but again not an overly bright, overbearing one. For this first layer I used a crimson red and black.

6 Blend your colors together using a colorless blender or a white colored pencil. Darken up any colors you need to after the blending, such as the red, then add some scales.

TIP: DON'T PRESS TOO HARD WITH THAT GRAPHITE PENCIL!

Remember, if you are going to continue working on the same original drawing, make sure you plan ahead and don't press hard when doing the initial circles, or they will leave little indents in your paper. If you plan to copy your drawing onto a new piece of paper, it is still good to press lightly, as you don't want your outline taking over your drawing (unless you are going for a boldly outlined style!).

THE DRAGON HEAD: FULL SIDE VIEW

When drawing a dragon's head either partially sideways or fully sideways, you can determine the shape of the head with the shape of your starting circles. If the skull circle is really large and the nose circle really small, but they are not too close together, your dragon is going to have a larger, blockier head. A nose circle that is maybe only a quarter as small as the skull circle, and placed far away, will make a long, narrow head.

The steps to drawing a dragon's full side profile are similar, but simpler, than the previous dragon head we just drew, so let's make this one a bit different by drawing the dragon with its mouth open.

1 Start with the large circle for the skull, but instead of drawing a smaller circle for the nose, draw two pieces of the mouth. They should be triangular but flattened on the end of the nose. Position the ear and neck. For this dragon, draw the ear quite high up on the head, similar to how a horse's ear is positioned, with the neck arching downward. The top of the neck should also start behind the ear.

2 Start filling in some of the details of the face, such as shaping out the head, and adding an eye and tongue.

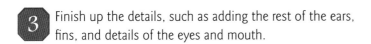

3 Finish up the details, such as adding the rest of the ears, fins, and details of the eyes and mouth.

4 Clean up your drawing or copy it onto a new piece of paper. Now that all the building lines are done, it is ready to color.

5 Add your first color layer, making sure to leave white highlight areas to show the curve of the neck, ears, and horns. In this example there are two shades of green, a brown, and a black.

6 Using a white colored pencil, blend your colors together to create an even, smooth surface. You can use a colorless blender for the darker areas, such as along the spine and on the dragon's fins.

Apply your last layer of color to darken up the shadows and brighten up the dragon. If you need to blend at this step, use the colorless blender so it doesn't whiten the image again. Finish the details, such as drawing out the scales, and you are done!

TIP: SHADING CLEANLY

To avoid messing up your drawing, shade from left to right if you are right-handed, or from right to left if you are left handed, like I am. This way, your hand won't pass over the completed sections of the drawing as much. For the same reason, it's also a good idea to shade from top to bottom.

DRAWING A DRAGON'S TAIL

What exactly makes up a dragon's tail? For the most part, it is usually just a really long appendage, like a snake's tail, on the end of the dragons' body. If there is one consistency among dragon body parts, it's that their tails are usually long and taper down to a point, although you can always give it a big, blocky end (we will look more at customizing the end of a tail in the next section). But, usually, dragon tails don't look like a horse's tail, or a lion's tail, or a fluffy little rabbit's tail (because that would be a bit strange, wouldn't it?).

The main thing to look at when drawing a dragon's tail is how you want to balance your dragon. Typically, if you are going for a cute, compact, little baby dragon with a short neck, you balance the shorter neck and body with a shorter tail. The same could also be said for a thick-necked, blocky, muscle-bound beast—you may not want that dragon to have a super-long, thin, winding tail.

Likewise, if you are trying to draw a long, air-bound Eastern dragon or an elegant, agile dragon with a long, arching neck, you can balance out the long neck and thin body by giving your beast a long tail.

Other than that, the main thing to focus on when drawing a dragon's tail is that it should continually decrease in width. I usually avoid giving the tail spots where it widens part way down the tail, as the tail should be wider the closer it gets to the rump (with the exception of making a big blocky end on a tail, or perhaps a crocodile tail).

This dragon might just make your head spin!

Where does the neck end, and the tail begin?

DRAGON CLAWS

A dragon's claws can say a lot about the beast. Does it have large, catlike paws with large talons, ready to pounce on prey, or are the claws longer, more delicate, and more like human fingers? Regardless of these specifics, claws usually have a basic shape. In *Drawing Dragons*, I looked at different types of legs, arms, and claws, so let's just focus on a few core poses here, with what I would consider to be a standard dragon claw (we will take a closer look at different legs and claws in this book later on, when drawing full dragons).

DRAGON FRONT CLAW: STANDING

Let's take a look at drawing a front claw resting on the ground with its fingers outstretched. (If I wanted to convert this front claw to a back claw, I might just make the claws a little longer and closer together, so they don't look like fingers.) This claw is sort of catlike, so if you wanted to make it look more like fingers on a human, you can make the fingers a bit longer as well.

   Although this claw is resting on the ground, you can alter this claw position slightly for a dragon stretching out its claws when not resting on the ground (we will do this on page 87).

1 Draw a circular shape for the main part of the hand, and then decide how you want the fingers/talons to be generally positioned. You can either make your starting lines rounded like this, or you could make them come to more of a point if you want sharper, pointier claws.

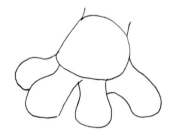

2 Within your basic claw shape, draw in the details of each claw and finger. These fingers are flattened on the bottom, as the dragon is resting the paw on the ground.

3 Clean up your building lines or copy your drawing onto a new piece of paper, and add some details such as scales.

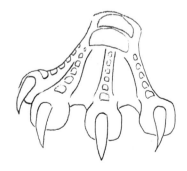

4 Add your first layer of color, making the color darker in the crevices and spaces of the claws, and lighter on the top so they appear round.

5 With a blender or white colored pencil, smooth out your colors, filling in the white space.

6 Darken up the crevices and shadows again with your chosen color (in this example, red), and your dragon claw is complete!

TIP: USING A MODEL CAN BE THE EASIEST AND SMARTEST THING TO DO

Many people find hands, feet, and claws to be a challenge, and sometimes you are really looking for too specific an angel or pose to turn to stock photos on the internet for your reference. So I recommend using a model. Take photos of your hand in the position you want, or of your dog's or cat's paws so that you have something to work with. (No people or animals should be harmed, though, in the making of your art!)

DRAGON BACK CLAW: STANDING

I usually draw a dragon's back claw to look a bit more like a foot rather than a hand so that there is a differentiation between the two. Here, I will try to draw the dragon's back claw a bit more like a dinosaur hind foot, where it is partly lifted off the ground and is sort of walking more on its toes. If you were drawing a back claw facing forward, for example, you could certainly alter the front claw to look more like a foot; in fact, that is exactly what I did for the dragon on the cover of this book! But, for now, let's draw a back claw facing sideways so you can see what I mean about it looking more like a foot.

1 Start out with a blobby-looking dinosaur foot shape. In the example, you can see the ankle is raised off the ground, and I've drawn toe shapes just to determine the length and side of the toes.

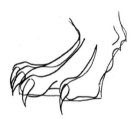

2 Now, work out the details of the toes and how many you want. Even though I only drew two blobby toes, I actually wanted this foot to have four toes. But as you can see, the first rough shape helped determine the overall length of the toes, and at this point, the claws as well.

3 Erase the building lines and add some scales if you want to.

4 Start your first layer of color. This time I applied more color to the top of the toes than the bottom, as I wanted the bottom of the foot to appear lighter, like the bottom of our feet usually are.

5 Blend your colors together with a white pencil or blender.

6 Once again, darken up the areas that you want more color on, such as the top of the toes, and add some details to the foot, such as scales.

DRAGON FRONT CLAW: RESTING OFF THE GROUND

Another common front claw position that I often find myself drawing is one that is resting off the ground. That is, the dragon's front claws are not on the ground—perhaps the dragon is flying or sitting back on its haunches. Either way, it isn't a pose that suggests the dragon is stressed or angry, such as when the claws or talons are stretched out. I also find this claw pose usually looks a bit more human, so you can always use your own hand as a model, which is, well, handy!

1 Draw a circular shape to start your hand (or would you say this is just a triangle that wishes it were a circle?), and draw claw-like fingers coming down. Depending on what side you are facing, you may also draw a thumb, such as in this example.

2 Fill in the details of the fingers, thumb, and nails. Again, this is a good one to have a hand model for, or take a photo of your own hand to use!

3 Erase your building lines and add some scales. I find plated scales really look best on fingers because of all the joints and the knuckles.

4 Apply your first layer of color. The color should be darker on the top than the bottom, so that the underside of the fingers and palm have more white space.

5 Blend your colors together and into the white areas left on the fingers and palm, so that the color transitions naturally into those areas.

6 Darken up the colors and scales. In this example, I also added a bit more of a lighter, lime-colored green to transition the darker green to the underside of the claw.

DRAGON WINGS

There is no denying that wings are usually an integral part of a dragon. Although not all dragons have wings (such as most Eastern dragons who fly using magic rather than appendages on their body), most classic Western dragons do. Even when drawing other types of dragonish beasts, you can certainly add wings or wing-like things to them to add some character!

The first point you need to consider when drawing dragon wings is, how big are they? If you make the wings too small, they won't actually be feasible for a dragon to fly with. Also, the larger the dragon, the larger the wings actually need to be. Consider the examples below. We have a dragonfly, humming-bird, bat, sparrow, eagle, and heron. You will notice that the larger the animal gets, the larger the wings get. A dragonfly appears to have quite large wings, but its actual body size and weight are very small.

Also, the larger the wings, the more the dragon can soar over rooftops and clouds, whereas a small hummingbird or even a sparrow must beat its wings very quickly to fly. So if you don't picture your dragon frantically beating its wings to stay afloat, but rather soaring gracefully above the trees like an eagle, then you will want to give your beast a longer, larger wingspan.

Of course, you also need to think about how big your drawing is going to be, as giant, stretched-out wings can take up a lot of space!

The last consideration is where to position your dragon's wings. Even though many dragons also have front legs or arms, the wings still need to come off the dragon's shoulders in order to look viable for flying. If the wings are too high up on the neck or too far down the back, there is no muscle to actually move the wings, and your dragon is going to look strange and unfeasible.

Let's take a look at a few poses for drawing a classic, bat-like dragon wing, and then try doing a few variations of the types of wings you might want to give your huge, flying beast.

FULLY EXTENDED

This is a great pose when drawing a dragon in the air or taking off, and it shows the full wing. It can, however, take up a lot of room!

1 Draw the first part of the wing in a similar fashion to an arm, as if the arm is raised up and outstretched. The first point where it folds is the wing's elbow, and the second part where the wing fans out is the wrist. In *Drawing Dragons*, I included a wing with four fingers fanning out from the wrist, so this one is more similar to a bat's wing, with only three fingers fanning out, plus an extra spine I usually like to add down by the wing's elbow.

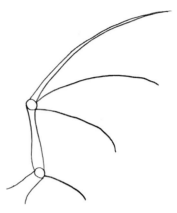

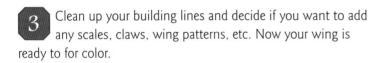

2 Finish adding the spines (or fingers) to the wings, making sure not to make them too thick. Then connect each spine with a curving line that turns inward. In front of the wing, add a membrane between the wrist and the shoulder as well.

3 Clean up your building lines and decide if you want to add any scales, claws, wing patterns, etc. Now your wing is ready to for color.

TIP: DIRECTION MATTERS WHEN BLENDING

When blending your colors together, try to blend from the darker areas to the lighter ones with small, careful strokes. Make sure you don't pull the darker colors too much into the lighter areas as this will cause streaking and ruin your highlights. For example, when blending a neck, start with the darker colors but move down the neck carefully so you don't end up with streaks of the blended color going too much into your highlights. This can quickly make your dragon look flat rather than three dimensional. If this happens, you can blend in a circle pattern over the lighter areas with your white pencil to try and smooth out the area again.

4 Choose your color and start building it up, shading the corners by the wrist and along the spines darker to make the spines stand out.

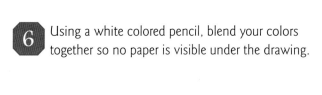

5 Add another lighter color. In this case, I added a lighter lime green, and also a bit of black to really darken up the corners before I blend them all together.

6 Using a white colored pencil, blend your colors together so no paper is visible under the drawing.

7 Add a bit more color to the corners and where the white lightened your colors up too much. I added more of the lime green in the middle of this one, as well as more of the darker green to the corners. Add any scales or patterns you want, and your wing is done.

PARTIALLY FOLDED DOWN

If you need a bit more space on your page to draw the rest of your dragon than a fully outstretched wing allows for, a partly folded down wing might be just the answer to your problem!

1 Start the wing like a raised arm going up, and then draw some sweeping lines curving downward, as shown. These will become the spines on the wings. Because these wings are relaxed, but not completely folded up, they will arch in a bit more than the stretched-out wings do.

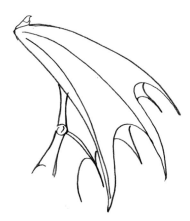

2 Clean up your building lines. Choose your color and begin adding your first layer to the wing, with the darkest coloring under the wing.

3 Add another layer of color and darken up your shadows.

4 Blend your colors together. Darken up your colors, adding a bit more red and orange so that the wing doesn't appear pink.

FOLDED DOWN RESTING

When not in flight or actively stretching, a dragon's wings will often be lowered, resting against their body.

1 We are going to draw the wing facing downward, but still bent back a bit. Draw your spines sweeping out from the wing's wrist again, but this time, don't fan the wing out. Connect your spines to create your wing's webbing, but rather than drawing them tightly attached, draw extra fold lines in the wings and give them lots of drooping slack between the end of each spine.

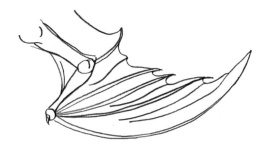

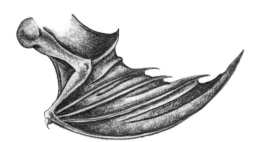

2 Clean up your building lines and choose your color. Begin adding your first color layer to the wing, with the darkest color near the corners and near the spines.

3 Add any other colors you want. In this case, I added a brighter blue and darkened the crevices with black.

4 Blend your colors together to create a smooth, even texture. Darken up any areas where you want to add more color after blending, and add scales to your wing.

FINLIKE WINGS

Let's take a look at a few alternative dragon wings you can draw. This particular wing style is great when drawing sea serpents or ocean-dwelling beasts.

1 Start the wing the same way you would a classic dragon's wing, with a long extended arm; however, this time skip the wrist, and extend the spines from the actual shoulder. Then connect your spines together.

2 Clean up any building lines. Add your first layer of color. In this example, the first color is red, and I added a bit of a pattern to the wings.

3 With this layer of color, the pattern on the wing really starts becoming visible. Here, I have added orange and a darker brown to make the shadows pop and also to really define the pattern.

4 Blend the colors together with your white pencil. Don't worry if the pattern becomes less obvious, as you can darken that up later. Make sure to blend in a way that doesn't completely ruin the pattern, however.

Reapply the oranges and browns to the darker areas of the wing so they are vibrant again and contrast nicely with the lighter areas.

INSECT WINGS

When drawing tiny fairy dragons, you may want to give them insect wings. This can add some interest to your dragon and set it apart from its larger cousins. There are so many different insect wing types to choose from that deciding between them might be your biggest challenge!

1 Start with an armlike appendage for the wing, as the wing needs a sturdy way to connect to the dragon's shoulder. The difference with this wing, though, is that rather than bending like a human or bat arm, it arches upward, almost like the elbow is bending out rather than in. The spines are also going to connect to evenly distributed spots on the top part of the wing's arm, as shown here.

2 Clean up any building lines and add a pattern to the wing. In this case, I used a dragonfly wing as a reference. Add a bit of shading inside the segments on the wings.

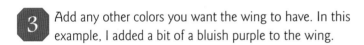

3 Add any other colors you want the wing to have. In this example, I added a bit of a bluish purple to the wing.

4 Blend your colors together, making sure not to completely blend your purples into your blues. If you want the wing to have a lighter color, you can stop at Step 3. I wanted to darken the wing up a bit in this example, however, and added a bit more bluish purple.

BIRD WINGS

The last dragon wing we are going to take a look at is a birdlike wing. You can also mix this style of wing with a more traditional dragon wing; for example, you could still add the spines with a bit of feathers in between.

1 The first step is creating a wing shape. Draw an appendage, somewhat like an arm, coming out from the dragon's shoulder, and then decide on the length and width of your wing. This example is based off an eagle's wing.

2 Decide on a color and add your first layer to the drawing. In this example, I actually added the darker color at the end of each wing, but you could also do it the other way around, emphasizing the shadows under the feathers.

3 Build up the colors on your wings, adding more shadows and darker colors to give the wings more shape.

4 Blend your colors together, even in the areas at the base of the feathers that were left white, in order to give them a bit of color. Add some scales to the arm to give it more of a dragonish feel.

DRAGON BODY TYPES

The basic shape of the dragon plays a huge impact on the overall feel of your beast. Is your dragon a long, lean, and agile creature, or one that relies on brute strength and compact muscle to catch its prey? Or is it neither, but rather a cute and cuddly baby dragon waiting for someone to bring treats?

Before you start drawing, you need to consider this basic shape. Of course, you can always modify your dragon as you choose, perhaps creating a long, stretched out dragon with a large belly, for example, but for starters, let's take a look at four basic dragon body types.

When starting a full dragon layout sketch, use simple shapes and start with the head first, then the neck, body, and tail. Those basic shapes will help you determine the body type and pose of your dragon, and will start bringing your creature (or creatures) to life, even before any detail is added. Remember to draw large, as well; it is easier to fill out a dragon that takes up a full sheet of paper than a tiny creature in the center of the page.

TIP: ALWAYS SKETCH YOUR BASIC DRAGON LAYOUT FIRST

Sketch out your entire basic layout first before starting details on a section (such as the head). The benefit is that if you are not happy with how it turns out, or with the pose so far, you can start again, as you wouldn't have spent too much time filling in details on any one part of your dragon.

THE BROAD, STOCKY DRAGON

First, let's take a look at drawing a strong, muscular dragon with a more compact, stocky build.

1 Start your dragon by drawing the head and neck. The neck should be somewhat short and thick, like a strong horse's neck. Connect the neck to another circle that will form the dragon's chest. Draw the chest circle larger than the circle for the head. The next circle will be for the rump and should be smaller than the chest circle. Attach the chest and rump circles with curving lines (think of how a back and belly curves). Finally, start the tail wide and slowly bring it to a fine point.

2 The arms should attach near the center of the chest circle and the back legs near the center of the back circle. Use circles to create your dragon's joints, such as elbows, knees, and ankles. Start the wings by attaching them to the shoulders. This dragon's wings are similar to bat wings. Again, draw circles for the wing's joints.

3 The last step to building the basic shape of your full dragon is to fill in details such as the claws, ears, and spines. Because this is a broad, strong dragon, draw the dragon with shorter, stubbier toes. Don't worry about finer details right now, just focus on the basic shape and positioning, and how the dragon is going to be standing on the ground.

4. Now it's time to start filling out some of the details of your dragon. Always start with the head, as ultimately, it is the most important feature of your dragon. Focus on positioning the eye and mouth. Flesh out the shape of the wings, arms, and legs. This dragon has very strong, thick arms and legs, so make sure to add muscle definition. Finally, fill out the details of the feet and claws. This dragon's hands and feet are short and thick, with large claws, as small, dainty claws wouldn't match the rest of his body.

5 Now that you have your details planned out, you can either erase your building lines, or copy your drawing onto a new piece of paper. The cheapest way to do so is to hold your drawing up to a window when it's light outside, but a light table works easier (see page 5).

6 Decide what color you want your dragon to be and start shading. Start with the head, shading around the muscle definition in the neck, body, and tail to start giving your dragon shape. Also, start building up your shadows. Here, I added black first, as it is a black dragon, but it could be a black-green dragon or a black-blue dragon—whatever you want! Start filling in the color in the wings and around the muscles. Be careful not to fill in too much, though. You want to leave enough white to give the muscles shape and not appear flat.

7 This is the blending step to smooth out all the color you have added. This drawing is mostly blended with a white pencil, as it smooths the colors out while still letting the muscle highlights show through.

8 Now that the drawing is blended, you can reapply the colors where you need to and darken up the shadows. Lightly draw the dragon's scales with a sharp, black colored pencil. This black dragon is relaxing in the cool marshes.

THE LONG, LEAN DRAGON—WESTERN

We are going to take a look at two different long, lean body types. For starters, let's take a look at drawing a traditional, winged, Western dragon with this shape.

1 Start with a circle for the head. This will be a dragon with an open mouth, so draw two rectangular shapes for the top and bottom of her mouth. Draw a long, curving neck, and a chest circle that isn't much larger than the head circle. Next, draw the rump circle far away from the chest circle. Connect the two circles with curving lines and finish off with a long tail.

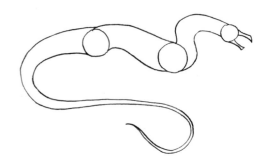

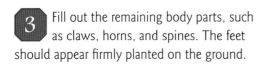

2 Add legs to your dragon. You don't want this dragon to look like a giraffe, so even though her body is quite long, the legs and arms should be less so. Draw some wings folded tightly down.

3 Fill out the remaining body parts, such as claws, horns, and spines. The feet should appear firmly planted on the ground.

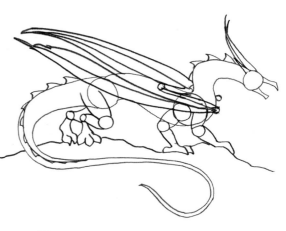

4 Start filling out the details of the face and neck, and fill out any details of the dragon's wings and body. Work out the shape of the legs, arms, and feet, adding muscle definition to them.

5 Copy your rough copy onto a new piece of paper to produce a clean, easy-to-color finished line drawing, or erase your building lines.

6 Start with your darker base color, in this case a dark green, and shade in the shadowed areas and around the neck and tail to help them appear round. Use a brighter green over the dark green base color.

7 Now it's time to blend the colors together! The white nicely blends the two greens together and gives the dragon's body a nice sheen and shape.

8 The final step is to darken up the areas that were lightened up too much when blending with the white pencil, and add some final details, such as scales. Add a bit of a background so your beast has a setting, such as preparing for a hunt on the edge of a cliff.

TIP: COPY YOUR SKETCH ONTO NEW PAPER

There are many benefits to copying your drawing over to a new piece of paper. First, all the building lines are definitely gone, as even when erased, they can still indent the paper. (If you are not planning to copy your drawing, use an H or HB pencil while sketching and make sure to press very lightly. That way, your lines will erase cleanly.) Second, you can easily tweak and alter aspects of your dragon as you go, such as changing the wing tips, length of the nose, etc. Third, if you start coloring and don't like how it's turning out, you can just copy it again and start over. Finally, I like keeping my building sketches, sort of like concept art or a rough copy, as it's neat to see the sketch compared to the final piece. You might also like doing the same!

THE LONG, LEAN DRAGON—EASTERN

Now that we've taken a look at drawing two types of Western dragons, let's take a look at what form an Eastern dragon takes! Eastern dragons are usually depicted as long, serpentine beasts, with short legs and eagle claws. They are typically benevolent and use magic to fly, so have no need for wings. You'll learn more about drawing Eastern dragons in Section 4.

1 Start your dragon with circles for the skull and nose. Next, draw a really long, snakelike body. Then, add circles for the chest and rump in order to place the arms and legs later.

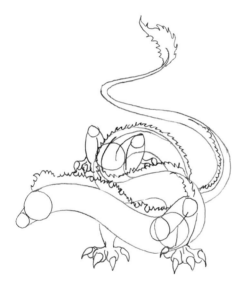

2 Place the legs on the dragon. This can be tricky since their bodies are so long, which is why you added the circles to help decide where they should go. Their legs are usually short and bend upward, like frog legs. Add feet, claws, and any ridges you want to add to your dragon.

3 Start working out the details of the face. Eastern dragons usually have some sort of beard and long, branching horns that point backward. Their face is usually shaped more like a lion's, with long whiskers. Finish fleshing out any other details, as well as shaping the arms, legs, and claws.

4 Clean up your building lines or copy your drawing onto a fresh piece of paper, and add some more details, such as scales.

5 For the first color layer, choose the darker color you want to work with. In this example, the base color for the dragon's body is actually gold.

6 If this dragon is indeed going to look golden, you need to brighten it up! Add some orange and a bright golden yellow to the dragon's body, and then some darker red-orange to the beard, spinal ridge, and tail.

7 Blend your colors with a white colored pencil. This step really dulls the dragon's colors, but the creamy texture the white blending creates will make it super easy to give the dragon a nice scaled effect next, so don't worry that it is lightening everything up.

8 After blending, apply another coat of the gold, orange, red-orange, and yellow to brighten everything up again. Then, take the white and fill in little circles in each scale (you should be able to just barely see the lines you drew in Step 4) to make the scales pop out. Add a bit of background, and your Eastern dragon is finished!

THE CUTE, COMPACT DRAGON

The last body type we are going to look at is a cute, compact dragon. The idea is to portray the dragon as small. Not necessarily a baby dragon, but just small and cute—like a kitty, but not a kitty.

1 The trick to drawing this body type is to make the head much larger, and the neck and tail shorter. When drawing this dragon, make the skull circle just as large as the chest and rump circles, and draw them all close together.

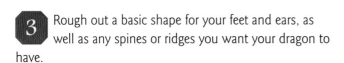

2 The wings don't have to be huge for this body type. A smaller wingspan will help create the look of the dragon being small in size, like smaller flying animals.

3 Rough out a basic shape for your feet and ears, as well as any spines or ridges you want your dragon to have.

4 Start working out the details of the face and neck. Because this dragon is small, the eyes should be quite large. Finish up the shape of the dragon's wings and fill out the details on the legs and arms. Finally, draw claws on the hands and feet, and finish up the shape of the dragon's fingers and toes.

5 Clean up your building lines or copy your dragon onto a new piece of paper.

6 Start with a layer of dark blue, making sure to leave highlights on the arms, legs, neck, and tail so that they appear rounded and not flat. Add more of a lighter blue to the rest of the dragon's body, making sure to also leave white areas so that the dragon will have nice, bright highlights when you blend the colors together.

7 Using a white colored pencil, blend the colors together so that none of the paper shows through. As you can see here, the two blue colors blend together well, and create a nice highlight and great shape to the dragon's body.

8 Darken up some of the shadow areas that were lightened up too much by the blending. Take one of the medium shades of blue to draw scales on the dragon, then use a white colored pencil to draw circles in the scales to create highlights. Add a bit of background for your little dragon friend to play in, and you are finished!

PUTTING IT ALL TOGETHER

We have now gone over all the basic body parts and different body shapes a typical dragon can have, although your options are only limited by your own imagination!

Let's draw one last dragon, putting together some of the steps we've covered, before we move onto the next section. We are going to draw a dragon with a broad, stocky form, but with the head and chest facing the viewer. It will be similar to the front-profile head tutorial on page 16, but with the head tilted downward more. This will be a slightly more complicated pose than the side–profile pose we did in the broad and thin Western dragon examples, so don't get discouraged if it takes a few tries!

1 Build your basic dragon shape starting with the head, a nice large chest circle for our strong dragon, and a smaller rump circle. We want this dragon to be in its peak adult health, so don't have the belly sag too much between the chest and rump.

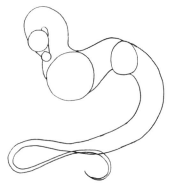

2 Add the dragon's arms and legs, and decide how you want to pose his wings. Because this dragon will face you a bit (the front of his chest will be visible), draw the wings fanning out on either side of him.

3 Finish your basic dragon layout by adding basic feet shapes, and any ears, horns, or spines you desire.

4 Start working out the details of the dragon's face and chest. Its face is very similar to the face you drew in the front profile head example. The dragon's chest will face you, so as you draw the underbelly scales coming down the neck, let them extend past the chest circle you drew earlier to make the chest wider on the left. Flesh out the shape of the wings and the joints in the wings, as well as the spines on the dragon's neck.

5 Fill out the arms and legs. Since this is a strong, stocky dragon, make sure to give them good, curvy muscle definition. Fill out the details of your dragon's feet, claws, and spines.

6 My sketch was pretty messy, as they pretty much always are, so I copied the drawing onto a new piece of paper using a light table. This allowed me to change the shape of the face a bit and really clean up the lines before starting to color.

7 You are finally ready to color this huge beast! For this dragon you can see I used two shades of red, using a bright red on the body and part of the wings, and a deeper red on the top of the wings and underneath the part folded down. I also used black for the shadows and spines, and a red-orange on the back fins. Don't forget that when shading with color, you want to make sure to leave areas white so when you blend, the highlights will give the dragon's body and muscles shape and they won't appear flat.

8 When blending a red dragon, you would think you would want to use a blender, and not a white pencil; otherwise, your great beast will turn pink. This is not the case, as the purpose of using a white pencil over a blender is to create a creamy surface on which to layer your colored pencil. To prove it, I did the blending early on this guy so he really got pink. Talk about getting pink eye, this poor guy has pink body! I blended the top part of the wings with a colorless blender, and the body with a white colored pencil, and you can really see how the body color compares to the wings. But, you will also notice that the entire body has a nice, smooth, blended surface, which makes the next step easier.

9 Now that the dragon's first coat of color has been blended, it's time to color him up! Here, I've built up a nice layer of the brighter red, as well as added a red-orange and lighter orange to the fins on his back. There is still a bit of pencil texture visible on his body and fins, but now that I've already blended with the white colored pencil, I can blend that in the next step using a colorless blender.

THE FINISHED MASTERPIECE!

10 I blended the last coat of color with a colorless blender so that the red stayed bright red, and then added a subtle layer of scales to his body using a darker red. To finish up your dragon, you can add a full background, such as this sunset, or you can add a partial background, as I did in the previous tutorials in this section. Either way, your dragon is sure to look splendid!

TIP: SCANNERS, PRINTERS, AND PHOTOCOPIERS CAN BE GREAT TOOLS

The original sketch for this red dragon took a few tries, but something was not quite right with him, which I couldn't place. I put him down for a week or so. When I picked the sketch up again, I realized his head was too small for his big body! But I really LIKED the head just the way it was, so I didn't want to erase it and try to draw another one. Instead, I scanned the sketch, then printed it and increased the size just a bit, by about 10%. Then, when I went to draw the dragon onto a new piece of paper to begin coloring, I started with the head and neck I had scanned and printed, removed that printed sketch from under my drawing, then put the original sketch underneath to copy the rest of the body in its original size. Voila, I had the right size head without having to redraw it. You could do the same thing with a photocopier by telling it to print about 10% larger.

Section 3

CREATING DISTINCTIVE DRAGONS WITH PERSONALITY

Once you have mastered drawing different dragon parts, shapes, and body types, you can really start customizing your dragon to your liking by giving it many different and unique features. From wicked horns, fancy frills, or extravagantly patterned scales, the possibilities are endless!

In this section, you will also learn how to make changes to the standard body types by looking at different ages and some specific animal features.

Your choice of features can have a great impact on how friendly or menacing your dragon looks, or they may just be a reflection of the dragon's age or environment. Either way, have some fun in choosing what to add to your beast, and don't be afraid to mix things up a bit!

GIVING YOUR DRAGON
PERSONALITY AND EXPRESSION

Quite often, dragons will be depicted either as serene, gentle giants or gargantuan, terrifying beasts bent on destruction. Because in one case they are somewhat expressionless and in the other, snarling and roaring in an animalistic way, they often don't portray a certain personality so much as a state of being, such as relaxed or angry, for example. But what if you wanted to portray an actual personality type and an emotion other than "I want to eat you?" Let's take a look at some ways you can add personality to your dragon (that don't involve adding Cheez Whiz).

BENEVOLENT, KIND, AND HAPPY

When drawing a dragon to look benevolent and kind, there are several things you can do. First, what the dragon is doing matters. You probably shouldn't have it devouring a hapless knight, shelled from his armor like a lobster. Try to depict the dragon in a relaxed pose, or floating gently in the air. Then give the dragon softer features, such as shorter, blunter horns, large pupils, and nonthreatening spines on the neck, if any. You can also try substituting obvious scales for a more furry look, or just smooth skin. For example, this blue dragon looks happy; her mouth is smiling and her cheeks curve up under her eye in a cheerful manner.

SINISTER AND EVIL

Try to think of all the troll and goblin bad guys in cartoons, apply their features to a dragon, and you will have a nasty-looking creature on your hands! Give your bad guy mean-looking horns and spines, grotesque warts, uneven teeth sticking out every which way, and an unpleasant color. Swampy greens and browns are a good choice of color, although you can go with any color you like... I just don't recommend cheerful tones such as sky blue or buttercup yellow! An unfriendly expression will finish off your beast's up-to-no-good look.

DISAPPOINTED OR BORED

Although similar in some ways to drawing a relaxed, almost emotionless dragon, this expression shows a dragon that is not relaxed but rather unamused, such as our purple dragon here. Perhaps it is because she is not impressed with the choice of scale color nature bestowed upon her, or she is tired of being called a "Purple People Eater" by her peers (she should have a conversation with them about not bullying!). With her horns, spines, ears, and eyelids drooping and a long frown on her face, she clearly is not having a good day.

THREATENING, MENACING, AND ANGRY

For this personality, you don't want to just draw a dragon roaring at the moon or attacking prey—this dragon is specifically angry and threatening. Think of a food-driven, possessive dog warning another dog to stay away from its food. You can see the spines on this red dragon's neck are raised (like a dog raising its hackles), his ears are back, and his teeth are bared in a snarl. His expression clearly says, "Stay away from my lunch or else I will eat you too!"

ADDING GENDER TO YOUR DRAGON

Like other animals, most of the time dragons, are gender neutral—you can't really tell what sex the creature is. Think of snakes, lizards, and birds, for example. Unless you happen to know that the males have different coloration or features than the females, there is no way to know. And even in animals where you can tell based on, well, certain anatomy, unless you are specifically looking, you still may not be able to tell unless you try to look. Take tigers, for example. They are huge, powerful hunters, and even when face to face with one, it is probably hard to tell if it's male or female.

Or, if you look at dogs, some breeds are very broad and muscular, regardless of their sex. My dog is half Yellow Lab and half American Staffordshire Terrier, so she is very broad-chested and stocky, and because she has very short hair, she also appears very muscular and strong. People often assume she is a he. Dragons are sort of the same. You could assume the broad, stocky dragon on page 37 is a male, but it could just as easily be a broad, stocky female dragon!

That being said, how DO you give your dragon gender, if most of the time they are gender neutral? The key is to emphasize certain traits and characteristics that we actually attribute to humans. While a woman can be quite large and muscular, typically a man is going to be broader and larger, with more defined muscles.

Let's take a look at the two examples here. These dragons are like humans (or any animal where both parents raise the young, such as lions, emperor penguins, and red foxes)—they coparent, so having a baby dragon in the drawing doesn't actually help define their gender.

I don't think there is any mistaking which one is the mom and which one is the dad; again, that is because I applied features to each dragon that stereotypically apply to one gender or the other in humans. The female dragon has a long, flowing spine, and the ridges over her eyes imitate long eyelashes (a common trick used in cartoons to make animals look more feminine is to give them eyelashes!). Her features are softer and her muscles not overly defined, and if she was standing, I would make sure to draw a curvier figure.

The male dragon, on the other hand, is broad-shouldered with strong arms. He is less curvy and more solid. His face is shorter, there is no eyelash effect over his eyes, and he has a beard.

That being said, both dragons look like they could easily eat you if you messed with their kid!

All in all, how you want to add gender to your dragon, or if you even want to at all, is up to you.

ADDING AGE TO YOUR DRAGON

People tend to draw dragons in the peak of their adult life. That is when they are the strongest, fiercest, and most menacing, so it only makes sense to create an impressive beast with these qualities. So far, this book has looked at drawing dragons once they are full grown (even if their full-grown size just happens to be small). Let's take a look at drawing some dragons that don't fit into that age category.

HATCHLING DRAGON

When animals are first born, or first hatch, they often don't have a lot of defining features yet. Even human babies have that certain newborn look that only lasts a few weeks. Hatchling dragons are the same—they are so new that they haven't developed a lot of personality yet. However, there is no denying that they are adorably cute! Let's draw a brand-new baby dragon still making its way out of an egg.

1 Start with your basic compact body shape, and draw an egg around it. Draw a short arm and wing poking out of the egg, and then draw a piece of the tail sticking out of the bottom. Draw the mouth open like the baby dragon is calling for food, almost like a baby bird.

2 Choose a base color for your hatchling and its egg. Make sure to leave lots of white space on the egg so it looks like the light is hitting it, making it look round. In this example, I placed the egg in a bird's type of nest and added a bit of a cool, dark green to the hatchling so it would match with the clover leaves.

YOUNGLING DRAGON

Have you ever noticed how quickly babies grow and change? Animal babies can grow at a very surprising rate, and even a six-month-old human baby looks entirely different from a newborn. So what is the difference between a young dragon and a hatchling? Well, the main thing is that younglings usually have much more personality! They are small, playful, and always getting into things. They also start to lose that uniform newborn look. The young dragon we are going to draw would be in what I would consider the preschool age—still cute but starting to get a bit more independent, and able to get into everything!

1 Draw your basic dragon shape the same way as the cute, compact dragon. Because this dragon is still a baby, draw short, stubby arms and legs, and wings too small for the dragon to fly with. This dragon is a bit older than a hatchling, so she has new, sharp, little teeth and thin, sharp claws, almost like a kitten.

2 Begin coloring, but make sure to still leave some white areas where the muscles bulge out so that your dragon doesn't appear flat. Blend your colors together and add some scales and any other details. I decided to give the dragon a pattern, almost like camouflage.

TIP: DON'T OVERDO YOUR BLACK COLORED PENCIL!

Unless you are actually drawing a black dragon or a dark-colored dragon of any shade, you don't want to use too much black for your dark areas. This is because when you blend the black into the lighter colors, it is going to deaden the color and turn it more gray. That's why I used more indigo blue in Step 2 of the young dragon rather than just more black!

SENIOR DRAGON

We don't need to look at drawing a regular adult dragon, since we already drew several of them in Section 2. Let's take a look at the next stage of life—a senior dragon.

1 Begin your basic long, lean dragon shape. We are going to make this dragon a bit less windy than the Eastern dragon in Section 2, as he is old and a little less agile. Add your basic leg and arm shapes. This dragon won't have wings, but long, webbed spines that he has grown on his back over the years (this will allow us to talk about tattered wings even though he doesn't have wings!).

2 Finish planning out the details on your dragon such as antlers and beards. Because this guy is quite ancient, his antlers are broken and a bit gnarly. He has a long beard and some old battle scars on his face and neck, and the webbing between his spines is getting worn, tattered, and ripped. You could also give your dragon some missing, chipped scales or wrinkles to help him appear old. This dragon is old but wise, and has managed to keep all his scales on his body!

UNDEAD DRAGON

Let's take a look at drawing the last stage of a dragon's life—its afterlife! While most dragons probably get to die an honorable, natural death, that may not be the case for all. Whether resurrected by a powerful wizard or through powerful magic of its own, an undead dragon is not something you want to reckon with. After all, how do you kill something that is already dead? Since a zombie dragon wouldn't be much different from a really senior dragon (with perhaps chunks of skin and flesh missing—gross!), we are going to look at a skeletal dragon.

1 This dragon has no skin or muscles, so its basic shape is going to be different from our previous ones. The neck and tail are going to be very thin, as there are no muscles—only a spine. The body is going to be thinner too. Rather than drawing a chest circle, draw two shoulder plates. Draw the basic shapes of the arms, legs, and wings. Again, everything is going to be super long and thin, as there is no skin and muscle, just bones!

2 Finish adding individual bones on the spines, tail, and rib cage. In this case, I modeled the dragon's rib cage off a horse's rib cage. Finally, you can either leave the wings completely skeletal, or, as in this case, add tattered and torn webbing to the wings, just to make the dragon look a bit more interesting and to make it more fun to color. It is a beast that has been magically brought to life, after all. Decide what base color you want your skeletal dragon to be. Do you picture it being a yellowish, bone-colored terror, or something else? I wanted to do the dragon in silver and blue.

HORNS, SPIKES, AND ANTLERS

We've taken a look at ways to personalize your dragon by adding unique characteristics, such as emotion, gender, and age. But there are also many creative ways you can customize your dragon by adding physical features to your beast. Now we're going to look at several examples of features, starting with horns and spikes, but remember, you can always make up your own! (I also have more examples of each feature in my graphite pencil book, *Drawing Dragons*.) Let's take a look at several different features you can give your dragon.

The horns, spikes, antlers, or head plates you give your dragon can really make a huge difference to the overall look of your beast. Long, sharp horns pointed downward will give your dragon a more menacing look, antlers may give a more regal look, and a soft, rounded head plate may give your dragon a more protective, gentle look. Make sure you choose wisely, but don't be afraid to experiment with different things. You can always erase and try again!

STRAIGHT UP HORNS

These are one of the most common horn styles I draw on dragons. You can either draw them curving up, such as here, or reverse them and have them curving downwards towards the back of the dragon's head.

MULTIPLE SPIKES

If you really want to give your dragon an impressive, dangerous-looking head plate, skip the dragon ears and add several large, spiked horns sweeping backward from the head instead.

CURVED SPIRAL HORNS

These horns curve and twist upward. They are a bit more delicate and fancy than the straight ones, but still sharp and dangerous looking.

KNOBBY HEAD PLATE

This is a great choice for a dragon that you want to give a more gentle or protective look to.

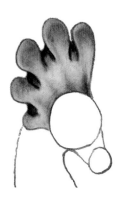

CURVED GOAT HORNS

These are smaller horns with an interesting shape, great for both large dragons and smaller varieties.

DOWNWARD-FACING BULL HORNS

These horns will give your beast a confrontational, aggressive look, as if it's ready to charge its enemy.

SPIRAL RAM HORNS

A unique horn type that can look good on any dragon, spiral ram horns can be quite menacing and dangerous looking.

ANTLERS

Antlers can come in so many different shapes and sizes, from sharp, branching deer antlers; soft, velvety, newly growing antlers; wide, flat moose antlers; or rounded, branching caribou antlers. I recommend using a reference for the type of antlers you want to draw. They are a great choice to give a benevolent dragon a regal crown upon its head, while still looking dangerous at the same time.

BACK RIDGES AND SPINES

Although it is common to draw a short, hooked spike along a Western dragon's spine, and a furry ridge is common on Eastern dragons, you can draw whatever style you feel suits your dragon. You can also leave the back of your dragon's neck and tail bare, with no ridged spine at all, which will give your dragon a sleeker look if it has smooth scales, or it could bring more attention to a rough, textured hide. Let's look at some classic types here, plus some more unique ones. You can always make up a new one too!

CLASSIC HOOKED SPIKES

These hooked spikes can be straight triangles, or they can be more hooked (like a cat's nail), such as these. For baby dragons, make the spikes more rounded, like little bumps.

FINLIKE RIDGE

This is one of my favorite back ridges to draw, as it is a little more interesting than the classic hooks and allows for more color variation.

WAVY HAIRLIKE SPINE

Most Eastern dragons will have a hair- or fur-lined ridge running down their entire neck, back, and tail. You can either make the strands long, like in this example, or make them shorter and furrier, like in the long, Eastern dragon body example in on page 43.

FEATHERS

You can really play around with giving dragons unique feathered spines. In this example, I drew individual feathers for each spike, but you could also do random or ruffled feathers.

LONG, THIN SPIKES

Long, dangerous spikes will give your dragon a more menacing look. You can choose to draw them all the same length or draw different lengths, as I did here.

SMOOTH FRILL

This large frill is a great choice for water and sea dragons, or even as a winglike frill on the back of a wingless dragon.

PLATES

Give your dragon a more armored, tough look by adding these plates along its neck, back, and tail. This type of ridge also looks good with plated scales!

FLAME

Ultimately, you can give your dragon any type of ridge you like. Maybe electricity shoots up and down your dragon's neck, or wildflowers adorn its back. This flame example would be a great choice for a fire or phoenix dragon! The choices are endless, so have some fun!

BEARDS AND WHISKERS

Adding beards, whiskers, and manes is a fun and easy way to give your dragon some character. Eastern dragons often have bearded manes around their head and long, twisty whiskers, but you can certainly give your Western dragon a bit of facial features as well. They don't have to be hairy looking, either. Let's take a look at some examples here.

GOAT BEARD

There is something that looks both wise and a little bit adorable about a small goat beard under a dragon's chin!

SPIKED FRILLS

This mane under the chin is anything but soft and fuzzy. Give your dragon a fierce beard with these spikes. You can create more than one layer of them as well.

SHAGGY, FURRY BEARD

You can make this beard thick like a lion's mane or a bit thinner. This one narrows right before the mouth before filling out again, but you can also make it thicker all the way under the head.

WHISKERS

Almost all Eastern dragons sprout a pair of long, curling whiskers from their nose! These can really add a lot of character to any dragon.

SPINY NECK FRILL

Great for any dragon, spines can face forward, such as in this example, or turn around and curve backward toward the neck.

SHORT MUSTACHE

This dragon mustache looks almost like it belongs on a short, mushroom-foraging beast!

MULTI-SPINED BEARD

These spines are hard and ridged, similar to the spiked frill, but they sweep downward and are made up of straighter spikes that follow a beard shape.

HAIRLIKE MANE

This is a bit different from the furry beards, as the hairs are long and thin and fan out from the back of the head. You can certainly have it extend further down the head toward the chin, and you could make the groups of hair more wavy, like the Wavy Hairline Spine on page 68.

SWIRLS AND SILLY THINGS

Although a beard full of flowers might make a strange sight, you can certainly come up with some fun beards of your own, such as a beard with lots of little braids ending in bright-colored bows, or these whimsical and funny swirls.

TAIL TIPS AND TUFTS

Another common feature of dragons and dragonish beasts is an extra something at the end of their tails! A common one seen on Western dragons is a pointed or spade-shaped tip, whereas Eastern dragons typically have a tuft of fur. Of course you can also leave your dragon's tail tip bare. Here are some more ideas for tail tips you can use, but you can also come up with your own.

TRIANGLE SPADE

This tail tip is like a spade, only more triangular. You can draw it perfectly straight or give it a bit of a curve, as shown here.

POINTED ARROW

This is another common tail tip on Western dragons.

FURRY TUFT

This thick, fluffy tail tip is common on Eastern dragons and usually matches their beard and the ridge along their back.

FEATHERED TAIL TIP

This feathered pattern could be drawn as the bulk of your feathered dragon's tail, or just as a feathered tail tip at the end of a long dragon's tail.

FRILLED TAIL TIP

This tail tip can be drawn either relaxed, like this, or with the frills more fanned out. A great choice for ocean and sea dragons!

SPIKED TAIL TIP

This tail tip can either be a continuation from a long spiked ridge along the back, or drawn alone. Also, you can draw the spikes with or without the webbing between each one.

WAVY HAIRLIKE TUFT

This is similar to the furry tail tuft except that the sections of "hair" are long and more defined, rather than looking like short, bushy bunches of fur.

SMALL LION'S TUFT

This smaller tuft of hair is great for smaller, furry dragons.

FAN TAIL TIP

This is perfect to give a more gentle-looking tail tip to your dragon. You could add some spikes to give it more of a defensive look.

FISH OR WHALE TAIL TIP

There is quite a variation in the shape of whale, dolphin, shark, and fish tails, so you might want to use a reference if you are going for a specific shape.

PEACOCK FEATHER

If you are looking to give your dragon or bird-like beast a fancier tail, look at different tropical bird tails for some insight, such as a peacock's tail feathers.

FLAME

Once again, you ultimately can give your dragon any tail tip you like. A wicked row of icicles might suit your frost dragon, or in this case, a little lick of flame might be just what a fire dragon's tail tip needs. Either way, you get to choose and design your dragon the way you see fit!

DRAGON SCALES

Now that we have looked at the different bodypart embellishments you can give your dragon, let's take a look at one part that is often an integral part of a dragon—it's scales! Of course you can also give your dragon a smooth, sleek hide, with no scales at all, or even cover it in fur, but for now, let's take a look at the different types of scales you can give your beast.

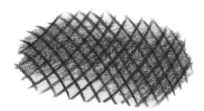

SIMPLE GRID

This is the quickest and easiest way to draw scales, and it is great if you just want to add the suggestion of scales to your dragon's hide without having to go into detail. I find this technique is best when drawing smaller pictures where you don't really have the space or even the need to draw out each scale. Choose a color that is slightly darker than the dragon's color so it doesn't take away from your drawing, but still shows up on the paper.

ROUNDED OVER GRID

When drawing this scale type, start out by drawing the simple grid, then round out each scale individually. Here you can see some of the grid underneath. Each scale is rounded out and then blended using a white colored pencil. This is a great technique for drawing larger scales.

FISH SCALES

Eastern dragons often have fishlike scales, although the scales can sometimes be a bit pointy, as is also the case with some fish! This style of fish scale has a very defined bottom portion, and again, you can see the grid was used underneath first to make sure the scales follow a grid pattern.

THICK, PLATED SCALES

These scales will give your dragon a more armored look and are great for large, broad beasts—or for little armadillo dragons, as well!

SMALL, CIRCULAR SCALES

A great choice for earth dragons or lizard dragons. You can make the circles all the same size or completely random sizes, or draw larger circles closer to the spine that slowly get smaller toward the dragon's belly.

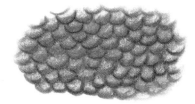

SMALL, CURVED, NON-GRID SCALES

These scales are similar to the rounded scales we drew over the grid, only the grid is missing and the scales are drawn freehand! As you can see, this means the scales have less of a pattern and appear more irregular and chaotic, perfect for sinister dragons who don't take proper care of themselves!

IRREGULAR ROCKY SHAPED

This is another great choice for earth dragons!

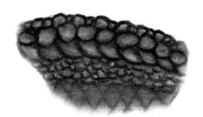

MULTILAYERED SCALES

Ultimately, you can choose any type of scale you like for your dragon, or leave your dragon smooth and sleek! You can also mix and match a few different styles you like, maybe starting with some rocky-shaped scales near the dragon's spine, followed by some small, rounded ones.

PATTERNS AND MARKINGS

Now that we have looked at different types of dragon scales, we can take a look at markings or patterns you may want to place on your dragon's hide! You can use the markings to replace scales, in combination with scales, or more sparingly to appear as tattoos on your beast. Try mixing and matching your patterns, and have some fun with them!

Just remember, the more markings you add, the longer the drawing is going to take to color. The green dragon on this page took forever, as I had to carefully color around each marking. Here are some ideas that you can try on your dragons.

DIAMONDS AND STRIPES

These are fun to draw and mix well with other shapes. Cut the diamond in half and elongate it to make pointed stripes, like on the dragon's wing on the other page. Fill them all in one color or leave the middle a lighter color for added detail.

CIRCLES

A great looking and easy marking, circles can create a pattern along the dragon's body or be placed randomly to look like warts.

ANIMAL PATTERNS

You can draw any pattern you want based off of animal markings—leopard, zebra, lion, snake. Choose an animal you like and find a reference to work off of.

RAINDROPS

You can either draw these all in one direction, such as on the green dragon, or alternate them, as shown here.

SQUARES AND RECTANGLES

Draw these in different sizes, all the same size, or, for a neat effect, slowly shrinking as you create more rows of the pattern down the dragon's neck.

ROCKS

These are similar to rock-shaped scales, only spaced out more, and again, you can follow a pattern in terms of size if you want to.

STARS

I've included these on the list at my daughter's request. She wanted crescent moons too! A great choice for a celestial dragon trying to blend in with the night sky.

SWIRLS

Who doesn't love swirls? They are fun and whimsical and can add a bit of charm to any dragon's hide.

FLAME

You can really add any pattern you like, and it can be fun to come up with new ones that suit your beast. Remember, it's fun to mix and match as well. This flame pattern would look neat with teardrops or circles, for example!

ANIMAL FEATURES

You may want your dragonish beast to look a bit (or a lot) like another animal, but still have dragon features. This is a fun way to create your very own customized dragon, and it is up to you how much dragon over animal you wish your customized creature to display.

BIRD DRAGON

The first dragon we are going to take a look at is a bird dragon. This beast will have fully feathered wings, with scales on her body.

1 I modeled this dragon after an eagle. I also didn't want this dragon to have a typical bird's tail, which is why it is long and tapered like a dragon's. Shape out the wings. This bird dragon has a few sets of underwing coverts—those are the groupings of feathers before the main, large feathers that make up the secondary and primary flight feathers. The legs bend backward and end in three-toed talons.

2 Start filling out the details for the underwing coverts, and add the eye, tongue, spines, chest scales, and tail tip. Refine the shape of the face and eye, add any feather ruffles to the wings and body, and fill out the details of the feet and claws.

3 Erase your building lines or copy your rough drawing onto a new piece of paper. This is a good one to copy onto new paper, as doing so allows you to really clean up the feathers in the wings. Add some scales to your dragon to help give her a look that is more dragon than bird.

4 Begin coloring your beast, choosing a base color and a color for the darker areas of the wings and body so it doesn't appear flat. This is a good time to add a pattern to the wings and body as well.

5 Blend your colors together but be careful not to blend your patterns completely away. Darken up your shadows and add more color where needed afterward. Finally, add a background to give your bird dragon someplace to be. Here, she is protecting her territory from a hapless knight who accidentally wandered a bit too close to her nest!

HORSE DRAGON

This next dragon is a horse dragon. You can make the dragon more or less horselike depending on your preference, but two of the defining features of a horselike dragon would be the shape of the torso and how the legs bend, so you should at least try to stick with those shapes. A horse's legs bend differently than a cat's or a human's arms and legs do, because of how short of a distance there is between their shoulder and elbow. Consider looking at a reference photo to help you with the proportions of the horse's body.

1 Begin with the basic dragon shape, starting at the head. The neck won't be as long as our classic dragon's neck, but the chest and rump circles will be similar in size. Add the basic shapes for the rest of the appendages, such as legs, wings, and horns. The horse legs in this example are long and thin. My daughter thought smaller wings would be better on this horse dragon, so she can probably glide really well coming out of a jump, but, sadly, she won't be soaring in the clouds with her friends until her wings grow larger. She's just a filly.

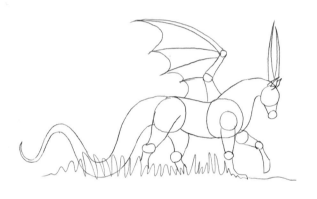

2 Fill in any remaining basic features such as chest plates, spines or frills, beards, ears, etc. Also place the eye, making sure it isn't too far down the face. Horses have long noses, but they don't have eyes on their nose! Add muscle tone and decide what type of feet you want your beast to have. I didn't want this dragon to look too horselike, so I gave her claw feet.

3 Clean up all your building lines or copy your rough drawing onto a new piece of paper.

4 Begin adding your color. I colored the dragon black, but with a bit of brown as well. While shading, make sure to leave some areas with white showing through, as done here, as this will give the dragon horse lots of nice muscle definition and help create a sleek, shiny coat when blending.

5 Complete the blending step. You definitely want to blend with a white colored pencil for this dragon, or else she won't have any nice highlights and will appear very flat! As you can see, the areas that had white from the paper still showing through brighten up with the white pencil to give the horse dragon a wonderful sheen. Finally, darken up the shadows, brighten up the colors on the spines, and add a colorful background for your horse dragon to explore.

LIZARD DRAGON

Drawing your dragon to look somewhat lizard-like is a great way to portray a smaller size, and also make your dragon appear more feasible as a pet. Lizards, like birds, come in many different shapes, sizes, and colors, so if you are hoping to have your lizard dragon look like a particular species (you know what I'm about to say here), use references, references, references.

1 I wanted this dragon to be sitting on a hill, so the basic shape is angled upward. This lizard dragon's face won't be really long, so the nose circle overlaps the skull circle. Add the dragon's basic appendages, such as legs, arms, wings, horns, and ears. Small lizards don't typically have strong, muscular arms, but rather, have cute, skinny arms and legs, so your basic arm and leg shapes shouldn't be too thick.

2 Work out the rest of the details of your lizard dragon, such as the details of the face, body, and feet. As you can see here, lizard feet have funny, long toes, so you may want to use a reference. (There is a close-up tutorial on doing lizard feet in my first book, *Drawing Dragons*.)

3 Clean up your drawing or copy it onto a new piece of paper. When I copied this guy over to a new sheet, you can see I was able to clean up his nose and face a bit more, and also add a circle pattern to his body.

4 Begin coloring your lizard dragon. I chose a dark green to shade in the darker areas and also used black for the shadows, claws, and spines. Continue adding your color. This time I added a bright, mossy green color on top of the darker green. I wanted his wings to have a subtle pattern, so I added some brown circles to the webbing.

5 Blend your colors together using a white colored pencil, making sure to color in small strokes on the wings. Don't go over the circles in long strokes, or they will lose their shape. Darken up any shadows that were dulled by the white pencil, and add a bit more bright green. I can almost see this guy grabbing a bug out of the air and munching on it!

FELINE DRAGON

Whether you want to portray your dragon as a powerful hunter; an agile, lithe creature; or a slinky, stealthy predator, using a feline as your basis for a body type can be a good choice. Like most animals, cats can vary quite a lot in both size and body shape, although they do tend to have more similarity between body shapes than some other animals (such as dogs, for example). Let's take a look at drawing a dragon using a lion's body shape, although any large, slinky cat would make a great model for drawing a catlike dragon.

1 Start your basic dragon form horizontal to the ground, and draw the neck thick and short, attached to a large chest circle. The tail should start out thick near the rump and then taper down to a fine point. Draw the rest of the basic body parts, such as legs, wings, and ears. The legs should be shorter than the horse dragon's legs and end in large paws, and the wings have many spines, as shown. Add the rest of the basic details, such as spines, beards, and in this case, some whiskers.

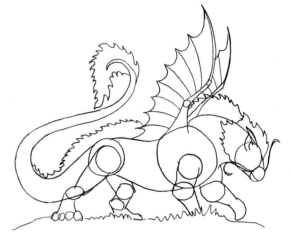

2 Fill in the rest of the details for your beast. I wanted the nose to be catlike, as well as the paws and claws. Add spines spread evenly along the wing arm for this style of wing, rather than having all the spines originate from the wing's wrist. Finally, add some muscle definition, markings, and scales.

3 With all the scales and markings on this guy, it was definitely a good choice to copy him onto a new piece of paper. If you do want to clean up your original drawing, try erasing all your lines (but not too much for the ones you are keeping, so you can still see them!) and then redraw over your partially erased building lines.

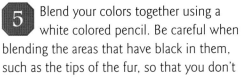

4 The base color for this dragon cat is a bright, true red, with some red-orange added to the spine and wings. Add some black to the shadows to darken up those areas. Then add bright orange to the body, and some yellow to the ends of the wings, spines, and beard.

5 Blend your colors together using a white colored pencil. Be careful when blending the areas that have black in them, such as the tips of the fur, so that you don't drag too much of the black into your yellow areas. Brighten up your colors again using bright red, orange, and yellow. I wanted this dragon to look like an Eastern-style dragon, which is why I gave him smaller, fanned wings and whiskers, and placed him in front of some bright Chinese lanterns.

BREATH WEAPONS AND FIRE

Of all the unique characteristics and abilities dragons have, perhaps one of their most iconic is breathing fire. I covered fire-breathing in detail in my last book, *Drawing Dragons*, but didn't delve into any other types of breath weapons a dragon may have. That being said, you can certainly give your dragon ANY type of breath weapon you like. My son Logan has a book called *Not Your Typical Dragon* about a young dragon that breathes out whatever is needed at the time—whipped cream, marshmallows, party streamers, Band-Aids—you name it! Let's take a look at six more common (and perhaps more realistic than party balloons) examples here.

FIREBALL

This example shows a classic fireball. It has a long tail as it streams from the dragon's mouth. Remember that fire is a light source, so to help make your fire look bright, add a dark background to your drawing.

FROST BLAST

You can draw a frost blast several different ways, such as having ice shards fly from your dragon's mouth, or, as in this example, draw a main blast with ice shards flying off of it.

ACID ATTACK

Don't get caught by this stinky, deadly attack! A great choice for swampy dragons and bad guys. Think of a cloud of murky, stinky gas when drawing this one.

FLAME STREAM

Unlike the fireball example, which has a main ball of fire at the end, the stream of fire is more consistent in appearance, with licks of flame curving off all along the blast's tail.

WATER JET

This attack will be sure to put out a fiery dragon's breath and leave it feeling soggy! The water spreads out as it gets farther from the dragon's mouth, leaving spaces between the water and water droplets.

LIGHTNING STRIKE

Like fire, lightning is a light source, so when coloring your drawing, you actually want to color behind the lightning bolt, leaving it pretty much white.

PUTTING IT ALL TOGETHER

Now that we have looked at lots of different, unique traits we can give our dragons—emotions, horns, spines, tail tips, markings, you name it—we can apply some of these features to a finished drawing!

For this tutorial, you are actually going to draw two dragons in a pose we haven't covered yet—fighting in the air! You will draw one in a more defensive pose and one in more of an attacking pose. Since we covered drawing different types of breath weapons, you will use those in your drawing too, and see how it turns out!

ATTACKING DRAGON POSE

1 This dragon is going to be in an attacking pose, higher above a dragon on the left, so position him in the top right corner of your paper (but don't forget to save space for the wings!). Because he is attacking, the beginning basic dragon shape consists of a lowered head, with the neck arching back. Draw a large chest circle and make the lines connecting the rump circle to the chest circle curve up slightly. Finally, curve the tail as though it is whipping around in agitation.

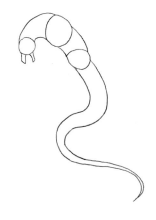

2 To save space, draw the wings up, but partly folded. The wings should be stretched back as the dragon lunges down to attack! Add the dragon's legs, arms, claws, and ears. Tuck the dragon's hind legs up out of the way, since he is going to be breathing fire, and throw his arm back as well, with claws out-stretched like an attacking cat. Lay his ears back against his head, rather than perking them upward.

3 Add the rest of the basic parts you want your dragon to have, such as horns, spines, and tail tips. Position the eye and tongue as well.

4 Fill out the details of your dragon, such as the details in the face and claws. I decided to give this guy a beard, as well as markings along his neck, arms, legs, and tail. Finally, plan out what type of breath weapon you want your beast to have. I went with a classic fireball.

5 Clean up your building lines or copy your dragon onto a new piece of paper. If you are going to copy onto new paper, I suggest skipping on to the defending dragon and planning him out as well. That way, when you copy them onto a new piece of paper, you can position them perfectly before beginning to color.

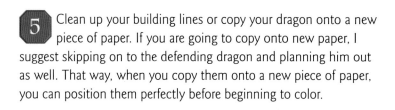

6 Add your first layer of color. To make this dragon dark blue, my first color was a dark, almost purplish blue for the under layer of color. Use a bit of black for the shadows, as well as a lighter blue for the spines, and a bit of bright yellow for the flames.

7 Add another layer of color. In this case I added two blues—a medium blue and light sky blue. Make sure to still leave a bit of white showing through in the highlighted areas so the dragon's tail and body won't look flat when you blend.

8 Blend your colors together. You can see here that once blended, the blue color really comes out, which is why I used a dark purplish blue at the beginning for the dark areas. Before moving onto the last step of coloring this dragon and adding a background, let's look at the next dragon in this drawing.

DEFENDING DRAGON POSE

1 This dragon might get the upper hand if he can snuff out the attacking dragon's flames, but right now, he is just trying not to get burnt by his older, more battle-experienced foe. The attacking dragon is in the top right corner, so this dragon's basic form should be drawn in the bottom left corner. His neck arches back as he fights back with a water breath weapon while trying to evade his attacker's fire. The tail is drawn flinging forward as the dragon lurches backward in the air.

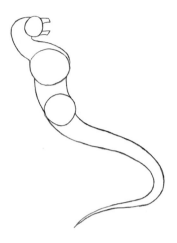

2 Draw the wings partly folded down to save space, and to give the appearance of the dragon trying to sweep his wings forward to catch himself as he flies back, away from his attacker. Add your dragon's legs, arms, and ears. Lay his ears flat against his head and stretch his hind legs and feet out in front of him to ward off attack. Add the remainder of your basic features to your dragon, such as horns and spines.

3 Work out the details of the face and claws, add any muscle definition, and position your dragon's breath weapon. I also started adding some chest spines and markings instead of normal chest plates in this step.

4 Clean up all those building lines or copy onto a new piece of paper, along with the other dragon. Copying this dragon onto a new piece of paper really allowed me to clean up the dragon's spines and perfect the shape of his head. Also, I was able to clean up the breath weapon nicely so it would really look like a water spray. Lastly, I decided to give this guy a bubbly pattern along his body and in the corners of his wings.

5 Add your first layer of color. I used a teal-blue color and black for the shadows, plus some bright royal blue for the spines.

6 It's hard to tell in this scan, but the next layer of color was actually a really bright teal. I also decided to add a bit more of the royal blue to the dragon's body, particularly in the shadows (instead of more black, as black would deaden the teal color too much when blending) and also to the ends of the wings to give them a bit of a pattern and shape.

CREATING DISTINCTIVE DRAGONS WITH PERSONALITY **91**

7 Blend your colors together with your white colored pencil. After blending the rest of the body, I used a white colored pencil with a nice, sharp pencil tip to emphasize the dots.

THE FINISHED MASTERPIECE!

8 Both of these dragons really needed the shadows darkened up with some black, as well as indigo blue for the attacking dragon and blue and teal for the defending dragon. Add a bit of scales here and there around the patterns on each dragon, and a hint of orange to the edges of the flames for the attacking dragon. Remember, fire is also a light source, so you don't want to darken the fire up too much. The last step is choosing what type of backdrop you want to have for your dragon battle scene. I am always a fan of starry night skies, which are fun and easy to draw and color. I have two dragon battle drawings in my previous book, *Drawing Dragons*, one in graphite pencil and one in colored pencil (in the color insert) with starry backgrounds, so check them out if you want to!

TIP: DOODLING IS A GREAT WAY TO RELAX

Doodling is fun and relaxing, and can be a great (or, not-so-great, if you're supposed to be paying attention) distraction when you need one. When I doodle, most of the time I end up creating very stylized, non-serious works that usually don't amount to anything. Sometimes I like one and will save it—I have a huge folder for keeping any potentially usable sketches and doodles. Sometimes I'll just finish the doodle as it is, not to be redrawn or reworked later. I'm not sure exactly how many dragons, unicorns, and other creatures I have doodled over the years, but I can tell you, it would be in the tens of thousands!

Section 4

UNIQUE DRAGONS AND CLASSIC BEASTS

So far we've taken a look at drawing several different body types of dragons, including Eastern and Western dragons. We gave those dragons age, gender, and special characteristics and features, and even drew more animalistic versions of them. But what about drawing some of the unique and classic dragons and beasts from folklore and mythology?

There are many well-known and recognizable beasts from fairytales and legends (and, of course, some that are a bit more obscure) that you can choose to draw. Let's take a look at some classic dragons, and some that are not so mainstream, while still adding our own touches to them.

WATER DRAGON

We have already taken a look at drawing a classic Eastern dragon, as well as a couple different variations (such as the senior dragon and feline dragon tutorials on pages 64 and 84). There are many different styles of Eastern dragons you can choose to draw that come from different areas of Asia, such as China, Japan, Korea, Vietnam, and Malaysia. The various Eastern dragons are typically considered benevolent creatures that can bring good luck.

Since most Eastern dragons use magic rather than wings to fly, they are typically wingless, although sometimes they will have spines or swirling ridges coming from behind their shoulders or beneath their arms. They usually have faces and noses that resemble those of lions or cats.

Although any Eastern dragon could be associated with water or the weather, since we have already drawn a more traditional one with fur, let's draw a dragon with features more adapted to the water.

1 To give this water dragon the typically long, snakelike body of an Eastern dragon, start with the head, and from there draw a really long neck that connects to a chest circle the same size as the head circle. The body is quite lean on this serpentine dragon, so the rump circle will be around the same size as the other two. You can also just draw a *really* long tail coming off of the head, and then add your chest and rump circles afterward so you'll know where to place the arms and legs.

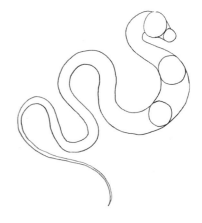

2 You won't be adding wings to this dragon, so the next thing to add are the arms, legs, mouth, and eye. You still want this dragon to look like a fairly traditional Eastern dragon, so make sure the arms and legs are small—not too long and not too thick. Draw in your basic claw shapes, and for the first specifically water-dragon feature, add webbing between the toes and fingers.

3 Now add some fins and horns. Where our traditional Eastern dragon had a furry beard, fur running down its back, a tufted tail, and branching horns, this dragon's more sea-creature look consists of finlike ridges running down his back and around his neck, a wide finlike tail (you could do a whale tail if you wanted to), and straight horns like a narwhal's. Don't forget to still give him whiskers, though!

4 Finish working out the details of your dragon, such as the fine details of his face, hands, and feet. Eastern dragons are often depicted either holding onto, or with, a pearl, which apparently is where they get their magical powers from. Does that mean if I can get a hold of an Eastern dragon's pearl, I will be able to fly through the air too?

5 Erase your building lines and circles, or copy your drawing onto a new piece of paper. Add some spirals to your dragon's narwhal horns and roughly sketch in a large grid for the scales. You will use this grid as your template when you draw the large scales later.

6　Begin coloring your dragon. Since this dragon is a water dragon, let's color him blue. I chose a vibrant royal blue, plus a bit of black for the shadows. Don't worry at this point about drawing out the scales, as right now, you just want to get the base color down.

7　Add another layer of color to brighten up your beast! Any bright blue or turquoise would look good on a water dragon. I chose a bright, light blue, as well as a light, yellowish brown for the dragon's horns. I also added a bit of a pattern to his back.

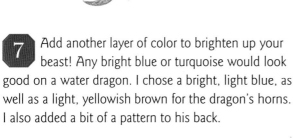

8　Blend your colors together to create a smooth look to your dragon, but be careful not to ruin the shape of the pattern on his back!

9　Finally, darken up the shadows and add glittering scales to your dragon. This water dragon looks like he would be as comfortable under water as floating above it. You can almost see how, if his neck and part of his tail were sticking out of the water, he could be mistaken for a sea serpent. Add a background for your benevolent water beast to play in, making sure that water is one of the main features, of course!

EARTH DRAGON

Now that you have drawn a fairly traditional Eastern dragon with some new variations in fins, horns, and color, you can draw another type of Eastern dragon with a totally different body type.

In Chinese folklore there are many different depictions of dragons, and they can take many different animal-like forms. They were often used to adorn different parts of Chinese architecture and objects, from the tops of roofs and the ends of swords to the tops of bells and on musical instruments. One such dragon is called a *baxia*, which is a large tortoise, or turtle dragon. It was said that the baxia liked to carry heavy things on its back. Let's draw our own turtle dragon as a huge and ancient earth dragon, carrying an entire forest on his back!

1 Start with your basic head circle and then draw two parts of a basic open mouth shape. Draw a neck curving down. From there, the basic dragon shape is going to change drastically—into a turtle shell shape! Draw a bit of the chest and rump circles poking out from under the shell. Finally, add a short tail.

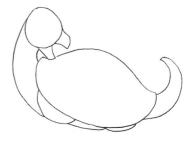

2 Add the rest of the basic body parts, such as the legs, mane, tail, and eye. A turtle dragon should have short, stubby legs with short toes.

3 Continue adding basic details to your turtle dragon, including his chest plates, the rest of his mane, small branching horns, and the beginnings of a pattern on his back. Leave a big splotch on the top of his shell to draw a forest on.

4 Fill in the rest of the details for your dragon, including the remaining pattern on his shell, and his face, toes, and claws. Then start drawing a small forest on his back. Don't forget the pearl!

5 This dragon had so much going on that it really helps to copy him onto a new piece of paper. If you can't do that, try erasing all your lines, but erase the lines you are keeping lightly so you can still see them, and then carefully redraw them more neatly.

6 Begin coloring your turtle dragon. Since this guy is an earth dragon, color him in earth tones of blue, green, and brownish gold. Use a bit of black to create shadows where needed, such as under the shell, belly, and neck.

7 Add some brighter colors in the next layer, such as a bright green to the shrubs and trees, some reddish-brown for the earth, and golden brown on the dragon turtle's mane, tail, and chest. I also added a slightly more vibrant jade green to his arms and body.

8 Blend all your colors, making sure to be very careful along the lines on his shell. You don't want to shade right over all the lines or they will not stand out. Instead, color between the lines with the white colored pencil, leaving the lines on the shell darker. Use small circular motions to blend smoothly between the larger spots on his shell.

9 Darken up your colors where they were lightened up too much by the white blending, and add some large, stylized scales to the earth dragon's legs, tail, and head. Add a background with some animals, such as deer or birds, to really portray the size of the ancient earth dragon as he rises from his slumber beneath the forest growing on his back!

AIR DRAGON

One of the dragons in my previous book was an amphiptere. An amphiptere is a long, sinuous dragon with a serpentine body and large wings, usually at least partly feathered, that has no legs or arms at all! They are typically green or greenish-yellow and like to wrap their tails around tree branches, similar to a snake, when landing.

For our air dragon, let's draw a more birdlike amphiptere who is more comfortable soaring and blending in with the clouds than coiling on branches in the forest.

1 Start your dragon off as usual, with the head first, followed by a long, arching neck. Because this dragon has no legs, you just need to draw a chest circle to attach the wings to, and then a really long tail.

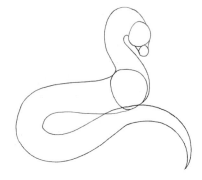

2 The next step is to draw the wings. Don't worry about working out all the details of the feathers just yet, but try to figure out the basic shape of the flight feathers and underwing coverts. In this example, I modeled the wings off of a swan's wings.

3 Fill in the rest of the basic parts of your air dragon, straying from a typical amphiptere that would have a snakelike tail and instead giving her a fancy, feathered tail tip and a full head plume of feathers. Draw your dragon's eye as well, and start forming a beak-like nose tip and mouth.

4 Fill in the remainder of your air dragon, such as the details of the face, chest plates, and wings.

5 Clean up your building lines and add some light scales to use as a guideline for scale placement later.

6 For your first color layer, choose a light, airy color rather than a really dark color as a base. In this example, I chose a light blue, with a golden yellow for the chest and circles on the long feathers.

7 Add a second layer of color, again avoiding anything too dark if you want your air dragon to appear light in color. Here I added a bit of darker indigo blue to the tips of the head and tail feathers, and around the yellow "eyes" on the peacock feathers. For a secondary color, I also added a light yellow over the body.

8 Blend your drawing to smooth out the surface and colors, but be careful not to blend your light-yellow hue into the blue, as you don't want her to turn green!

9 Add a bit of contrast to the shadows, but don't darken things up too much on this dragon. Add a background; in this case, a bright and sunny sky. Although this amphiptere has no legs, I think she would look great with long, heron legs and feet as well. If you decide to draw legs, remember to use references!

FIRE DRAGON

Although the typical Western dragon can breathe fire, not all dragons are what I would consider "fire dragons." Since we have drawn several Eastern and Western dragons throughout this book, let's try drawing a sort of Eastern-Western dragon mix, with features from both traditions. This will be a dragon who doesn't just breathe fire, she is partly made of fire! Hmm...perhaps she is actually part Eastern dragon, part Western dragon, and part fire elemental? Let's draw her and see what you think!

1 Start your dragon with the head and a long, curving neck. Since this dragon is going to be a sort of Eastern-Western mix, the body should be long and thin, but not as thin as that of the classic Eastern dragon, which is more snakelike. Draw a chest circle about twice as large as the head circle, and then a rump circle about the same size as the head circle, followed by a long tail.

2 Add your dragon's legs, arms, eyes, and ears. Make the legs and arms more like an Eastern dragon's: short and not overly thick, ending in talons.

3 Add a ridge of fire running down the dragon's neck, with a fiery tuft around the head and a fiery tail tip. Make sure to add little licks of flame coming off the fire so it doesn't just look like fur! Finally, instead of wings, give this dragon wavy, flaming tendrils coming out from her shoulders.

4 Finish working out the details of your dragon's face, arms, legs, and claws.

5 Clean up all your building lines, or trace your dragon onto a new piece of paper. Remember, if you don't have a light table, you can hold your drawing up to a window to trace, as long as it's still light outside!

6 Begin adding color to your creation. For starters, use a bright red for the base color, with some red-orange for the flames.

7 The fire dragon's color is now much more...fiery! I used a bright orange-yellow for the second color, applying it over most of the darker red and in the highlights. The combination creates a coloration very much like glowing ember!

8 Blend your colors together. As usual, do not worry about the white lightening up the orange, as that will be fixed in the last step. Now that she is blended, you will see the faintest outline of the scale lines underneath, which will help you draw individual scales in the next step and give them a bit of a darker shadow beneath each one.

9 The last step really brightens up the fire dragon! Using a bright red, I drew each individual scale. Then, to really soften each scale so the lines appear nicely blended, I used a bright orange-yellow to draw circles in each scale. This fiery dragon mama is busy taking care of the young ones while daddy takes his turn finding food to feed their hungry bellies. I don't think I would want to mess with this family, as even the little ones look like they would burn me to a toast!

FAIRY DRAGON

These delicate little dragons can be so much fun to draw, and can have so much variation to them! You can draw them with intricately patterned bat wings or with insect wings, such as dragonfly wings, bee wings, butterfly wings, moth wings—you name it! The variations of butterfly and moth wings alone gives you endless options for patterns and colors. Fairy dragons also open up a whole new world of backgrounds and settings to draw them in, since they are so tiny. Your fairy dragon could be dwelling in a garden, hiding in a hollow mossy log, curled up on a mushroom, or playing in someone's old boot!

For this tutorial, let's draw a fairy dragon with butterfly wings. I used a monarch butterfly and painted lady butterfly as references for the pattern.

1 Fairy dragons are typically long and lean, so start your basic shape with a small head, a long, elegant neck, and long tail. Remember, even though these dragons are tiny, they are not babies, so you don't want to draw everything short and stubby (unless you are drawing a baby fairy dragon, of course)!

2 Next, add the wings, keeping the dragon's angle in mind. This dragon is going to mostly face sideways, so the pair of wings on the dragon's right side should appear thinner, as they are angled back a bit rather than facing perfectly forward.

3 Next, add the rest of the limbs, such as the arms, legs, and ears, and position the eye. This dragon is hovering in the air with her arms tucked in.

4 Draw the rest of the appendages, such as horns and spines, and fill in the chest plates. Start drawing the details of the face and mouth as well. This fairy dragon's horns are actually more like insect antennae!

5 Fill in the rest of the details for your drawing, such as the shape of the hands, feet, and claws, and what type of pattern you want to have on the wings. I also added a fancy frill to the bottom of the dragon's head to match the spines on her back.

6 With all the patterns, this drawing really needed to be copied onto a new piece of paper! When done copying it over, I finished the pattern on the wings and added even more of a pattern to her body. Now she's ready to color!

7 For the first layer of color, concentrate on one color per area. In this example, I used a dark brown for her body and around the pattern on her wings; black for her spines, antennae, claws, and outside border on her wings; and finally, bright red-orange for the pattern on her wings, chest plates, and pattern on her spines. Take your time, and leave some white space in the middle of each spot on her wing's pattern.

8 The next color layer will brighten the dragon up a bit before blending. Use a lighter, warm brown on the body, and add some bright, dandelion yellow to the wings. I also erased some of the orange on the spots at the top of the black border to make them more yellow. Add a bit of yellow to the spines as well so they are really multicolored.

9 Time to blend! You can really see how blending makes the drawing look much less busy. The details show up better on the body now, and the yellow blends in nicely with the orange. The colors do look a bit washed out as they always do after blending with the white, but it will be easy to brighten them up now that you have a smooth, creamy layer of pencil to work on top of.

10 Darken up the wings. I used a dark brown between the patterns again, and black on the wing borders. I also added a bit of black with a really sharp pencil to the shadows and lines on the body, before adding more orange and yellow to make the colors pop. Finally, to add scales that weren't too overbearing, I used a slightly darker brown to draw a grid over her body, and then took the white to draw small circles within each scale, which created that shiny, gently scaled effect. Once done, add a background. I didn't want to introduce yet another contrasting color to the picture such as green, so instead drew bright yellow autumn leaves, with a hint of blue sky behind them.

WYVERN

The main distinction between a wyvern and a classic Western dragon is that a wyvern only has hind legs and wings, no arms or forelegs. In this regard, they are somewhat more realistic (how many invertebrates do you know that have two sets of appendages coming from their shoulders?).

Let's draw a wyvern midair, perhaps getting ready to land after a long flight.

1 Start with your basic dragon form. This wyvern is going to be strong but not large and bulky, so draw a long, arched neck, chest and rump circles about twice the size of the skull circle, and a long, curved tail.

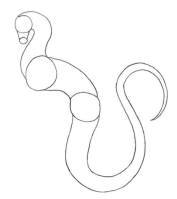

2 Since a wyvern has no arms, draw wings and hind legs only. Wyverns typically have large bat wings and large, powerful hind legs. Since the wings on this dragon take the place of arms, draw a larger circle where you would normally draw a wing's "thumb" joint. This will help to make this part of the wing appear more like a hand later.

3 Finish adding the rest of the basic body parts to your dragon, such as ears and ridges. Place the eye and add the spines to the wings. Again, you are going to make the spot where the spines attach look more like a hand, so think of the spines on the wings as long fingers.

4 Fill out the rest of the details of the drawing, such as those on the face and eye; the muscle definition on the body, wings, and legs; and the details of the feet and claws.

5 Clean up your building lines or copy your wyvern onto a new piece of paper. In this step, you will see how the wing looks more like a hand, and where the wing's spines attach like fingers.

6 Choose a base color to work with. I chose a medium green, with black for the shadows and claws.

7 Add a second layer of color to brighten up your wyvern! The next color I chose was a light yellowish green, as well as a darker emerald green that I used to add a pattern to her wings.

8 Blend your colors together using a white pencil. Be careful around the patterns so they do not disappear or streak into the lighter green.

9 Brighten up your wyvern with the light green again where needed, and use the darker green for the shadows and patterns on the wings. Add a bit of a pattern to the body and scales as well. For the scales, I drew very fine, thin lines in dark green, and then drew small circles with the white pencil to round out the scale lines and take away the grid effect. Finally, give your wyvern a place to roam! This wyvern looks like she belongs in a great forest, camouflaged among the trees.

DRAKE

This formidable beast is typically depicted as a wingless dragon with four legs. What it lacks in flight abilities, it makes up with strength. Although it can be depicted as somewhat lizard-like, it is much larger than a lizard and not a creature you would want to run into unarmed!

1 To draw a very broad, strong-looking drake, start your basic dragon layout the same way you would a stocky dragon, with a short neck, very large chest circle, and smaller rump circle.

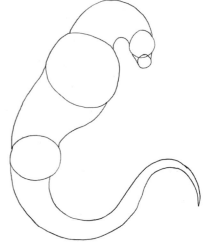

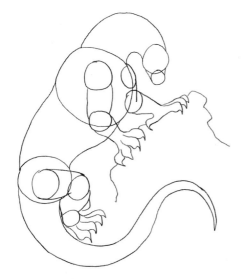

2 Next, add the basic shapes for the dragon's limbs—the forelegs and hind legs, as well as the beginnings of the feet and claws.

3 Add the rest of the basic appendage shapes, such as horns and spines, and start filling out the details of the face.

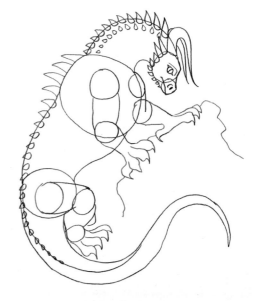

4 Finish up sketching the details on the drake, such as teeth, muscle definition, and details of his feet and claws. This drake is really strong and bulky, so make sure to give him muscular arms and shoulders.

5 Clean up your building lines or copy your drake onto a new piece of paper.

6 Begin your first layer of color. For this drake, I started with a dark brown for his body and black for his spines, horns, and claws. Leave lots of white space for the second color layer and to really give his muscles lots of highlighting definition.

7 Add your second color layer, in this case, a reddish brown and lots of spots! Don't worry if the spots look like they are too overbearing in this step—they will become more subtle once you finish the blending.

8 Blend your colors together using very small, circular strokes around the spots so that you don't completely blend them in with the other colors or create long streaks on your dragon. Leave some nice, almost-white highlights on his body, too, to help him look sleek and strong.

9 Darken up the shadowed areas that were lightened up too much, and add a bit more color to the drake's spots to make them pop out as much as you want them to. The less color you add to the spots, the less vibrant and obvious they will be. Finally, give your fierce beast a hunting ground to roam around in, as he looks eager for his next feast!

HYDRA

A hydra is a classic, usually wingless, multiheaded dragon. The difficult thing about drawing hydras and making them appear feasible with all those heads is that they really look strange where the necks attach to the body. I haven't seen a drawing of a hydra that I like, where you can see the whole body in all its strangeness. However, strategically drawn hydras that don't emphasize the chest area can be believably terrifying! So let's draw a hydra coming out of the ocean, looking for some poor seafaring fishermen to snack on. This allows us to draw the best part of a hydra—all those scary heads—without having to make it look like such a silly beast with tons of heads attached to one chest. If you decide to draw one out of water, try playing around with the position of the body and heads to make the beast look more feasible.

1 It's time to draw lots of heads! Decide how you want to position each head relative to the other. While you can have heads overlapping each other, try to think of your drawing as the perfect capture of a moment in that, if you were a photographer brave enough to snap a picture of this beast, you would want to keep the shot that showed all the heads clearly. So here, I purposely avoided overlapping them too much. The body has a line drawn through it to show where the waterline will be placed.

2 The hydra is underwater, so you don't need to draw its legs and arms. Draw one claw coming out of the water in the foreground. Start adding the spines and chest plates, eyes, and tongues.

3 Work out the rest of the details of your hydra. Hydras don't usually have ears, so instead I added some short horns to the side of the heads. Add lots of teeth and angry-looking eyes, plus splashing water so you will know where to color around the edge of its body coming out of the water.

4 Clean up your building lines or copy the drawing onto a new piece of paper. This one copied over nicely and gave me a good opportunity to really perfect the shape of each head. Add a bit of a pattern to your beast if you want. In this case, I covered the hydra's hide in a round, pebbly pattern.

5 Decide what color you want your hydra to be. For this example, I wanted to color the hydra in similar colors to an orca whale, so my first two base colors are black for the body and a yellowish-beige for the chest plates.

6 Add your next layer of color. I used a warm, bluish gray for the body, and a slightly darker yellowish-beige for the spots on the hydra's back.

7 Blend your colors together, making sure you are being careful when going around the circles. The black along the back of the hydra's neck should have been colored in densely enough not to need blending in this step, which is why the example still looks quite black here.

8 Finish touching up the colors on your hydra, and clean up the edges with a well-sharpened pencil. You can add scales if you want, but I thought the spots were enough on this one. Finally, time to color in the water and add a background! Use a reference when drawing water, and don't forget that water reflects colors, picking up colors from the hydra's hide. I wouldn't want to run into this great beast while out whale watching!

WYRM

A wyrm is typically much more like a serpent, with no wings or legs. However, they are much larger than any snake that exists today and can have characteristics that snakes usually wouldn't have, such as multilayered spines running down their back, or horns and spikes around their head. They move like snakes and are capable of lifting their head quite high off the ground with their strong, sinewy body. More animalistic, the wyrm is not nearly as intelligent as other dragons are.

1 The basic shape of this dragon is similar to the body type of an Eastern dragon, where no chest or rump circles are needed. Draw the type of pose you want, keeping in mind that the wyrm is going to have to hold itself up without the use of legs or arms.

2 There are no limbs or wings to add to this beast, so start adding the basic body parts, such as horns and chest plates, and adding details to the head as well, such as the eye and tongue. Then add spines along the back, and finish the shape of the head, face, and eye.

3 Clean up your building lines or copy your wyrm onto a new piece of paper.

4 Begin adding your first color. Leave lots of white highlights so that the wyrm's neck and body appear curved and sinewy, not flat.

5 Add a second layer of color. I chose a lighter green to build up the color on the body and added some brown to the horns and chest plates.

6 Blend your colors together to create a smooth, sleek hide for your wyrm. Be careful around the spines, being sure to blend with very small strokes so you don't accidentally blend the black from the spines into the green.

7 In the end, I added scales to the wyrm to make it look a bit more interesting. You could also add a unique pattern to your beast, based off a snake's pattern. There are some amazingly vibrant and beautiful snakes out there, although I don't think I would want to run into one this large, poisonous or not!

FURRY DRAGON

A furry dragon is exactly what it sounds like—a dragon with lots of fur instead of scales! Depending on the length of fur, you might be able to get away with doing bat wings, but since we've already drawn lots of types, sizes, and positions for bat wings, this dragon will have a more Arctic look, with long fur and soft, warm, feathered wings like a snowy owl's.

1 Start with your basic dragon shape. Since this dragon is going to be super furry, it shouldn't be too thin (Arctic creatures need lots of layers of fat and fur to keep warm). Even though you are not drawing a broad, stocky dragon, use that type of basic shape, with a large chest circle and a shorter neck and body.

2 Next, add the rest of the appendages—the wings and legs. This dragon has legs like a big, furry husky, with thick paws able to walk on cold snow. I used a snowy owl as a reference for the wings. Start with just the basic layers of the wing. You will fill in more details later.

3 Now it's time to add all the fur! As I mentioned, you are going to give this guy lots of long fur, suited for a cold, snowy climate, like I have here in Nova Scotia, Canada, in the winter. It usually snows here in January, February, March, and sometimes in December, just in time for the holidays! Start drawing the details of the dragon's face, such as his eyes, mouth, and ears, and add some curving horns.

4 Add the rest of your details. Yes, that means more fur! When drawing muscle lines on a furry dragon, that means drawing more furry lines. Even the feet and claws should have some fur on them. Finish the rest of the face, and fill in the rest of the feathers for each layer, with lots of small, warm feathers near the shoulder.

5 Clean up your dragon. This was definitely a good dragon to copy onto a new paper with all those furry lines everywhere!

6 Begin your first layer of color. I wanted this dragon to be white and gray, so the first color I chose was a warm gray, with a bit of black for the shadows.

7 The second layer of color on this dragon is actually a very light, cool blue, plus a lighter, silvery gray. This adds a bit of color to the dragon so he doesn't look like a black and white drawing.

8 Blend your colors together, making sure to use small, careful pencil strokes that move in the same direction as the fur.

9 Darken up any areas and shadows that you felt were lightened up too much by the blending step. This guy didn't need to be darkened up too much, but darkening up underneath each feather slightly, and in the shadows, gives the dragon's coat more contrast. Finally, add a suitable background for your furry beast. This one has a snowy winter wonderland to play in!

LAST WORDS

Well, that's it folks! I hope you enjoyed this book. Feel free to check out my previous book, *Drawing Dragons*, which covers drawing and shading using graphite pencil, and from which there is no repeat artwork here.

Remember, these tutorials are just guidelines and reflect my own interpretation of these beasts, so feel free to alter them to your liking, or even try combining them a bit. You might want to create your own fire-based, Eastern-style hydra! Either way, try to have fun, and don't fret too much if your drawings don't turn out exactly the way you want them to the first time.

Pretty much all of the drawings in the last section were drawn to scale for this book, so you can see exactly what the drawings looked like when I was done them. It can be daunting when browsing online to see such amazing finished pieces of artwork done by professional artists. I sometimes feel discouraged by them myself! But, remember, those are often HUGE drawings and paintings done in programs such as Photoshop, where every mistake can be easily undone, and then they appear amazingly detailed once shrunken down. Even the ones done in acrylic, watercolor, ink, and oil paint are often many times the size they are shrunken down to for books, comics, and online galleries. Hopefully, these drawings in their true size will help inspire you to do your best and not be discouraged by the fine details in pictures you see online and in books.

The key is to keep practicing, use references regularly so that you continually improve, and most importantly, have fun!

All the best...

Sandra

ABOUT THE AUTHOR

Sandra Staple was born and raised in Halifax, Nova Scotia, where she now lives with her husband, Jason, daughter, Chloe, and son, Logan. Her mother is a local artist, so Sandra has been drawing and painting since she was a young girl, earning distinctions in English and art in high school.

She graduated from Saint Mary's University with a major in computing and information systems, and a minor in creative writing. After graduating, Sandra worked as a business and systems analyst for 17 years before deciding to leave the corporate world to focus on her art. This book is the first accomplishment of this career change!

Sandra has also managed a very popular personal web gallery of her art since university, at www.canadiandragon.com. When not drawing or spending time with her family and friends, Sandra can usually be found working in her gardens or elbow deep in her fish tank.

Feel free to follow Sandra on her Facebook page, Dragon and Fantasy Art by Sandra Staple, on Twitter @DrawingDragons, on Instagram, or on DeviantArt.